SAMARIA
THE CAPITAL OF THE
KINGDOM OF ISRAEL

STUDIES IN BIBLICAL ARCHAEOLOGY NO. 7

SAMARIA

THE CAPITAL OF THE
KINGDOM OF ISRAEL

ANDRÉ PARROT

Curator-in-Chief of the French National Museums,
Professor at the Ecole du Louvre, Paris,
Director of the Mari Archaeological Expedition

SCM PRESS LTD
56 BLOOMSBURY STREET
LONDON

Translated by S. H. Hooke
from the French
SAMARIE CAPITALE DU ROYAUME D'ISRAËL
(Delachaux et Niestlé, Neuchâtel, 1955)
First English edition 1958

© SCM Press Ltd 1958

Printed in Great Britain by
The Bowering Press, Plymouth

CONTENTS

[5]

Contents

LIST OF ILLUSTRATIONS

(The photographs in Plates 2–6 are from J. W. Crowfoot's *Early Ivories from Samaria*, by the kind permission of the author. The remaining photographs are by A. Parrot.)

[7]

List of Illustrations

List of Illustrations

(With the exception of XVI, XXI and XXIX, all these illustrations are from original or unpublished drawings by M. Pierre Hamelin.)

FOREWORD

In the broken country about ten kilometres north of Nablus an isolated hill is visible. In order to avoid its ascent, the modern road to Galilee passing by leaves it on the right. This hill is 'the hill of Samaria', which, as we learn from I Kings 16.24, Omri, king of Israel, bought from one Shemer for two talents of silver. On it the monarch purposed to build a city which was to become the capital of the Northern Kingdom. He had chosen wisely. Samaria, standing at the junction of the main lines of communication, controlling several trade routes, possessed every advantage. It was a superb observation point, for in clear weather it was possible, from an advantageous position, to catch a glimpse of the Mediterranean. It was also situated in the midst of a fertile region of olive orchards and vineyards. With such advantages it is not surprising that Samaria was destined to play an important role in world-history. Already the envious eyes of the great powers were turned towards it on a stage where the two great empires of Egypt and Assyria, towering above the petty kingdoms powerless to maintain their independence indefinitely, strove for domination.

Of the kings of Israel, Omri, Ahab, and Jeroboam
II, were realistic rulers, capable, upon occasion, of
forcible strokes of policy. Although the judgements
passed upon them by the biblical annalists are harsh
and often justified, yet in fairness to them it must be
acknowledged that they exhibited undoubted qualities of statesmanship, diplomacy, and military ability,
which many a monarch might be proud to possess.
Archaeology, in enabling us to reconstruct the stage
on which the prophets Elijah and Elisha, Amos the
shepherd, and the enigmatic Hosea, played their
parts, has also shown us what great architects these
kings of Israel were.

Two centuries spanned the history of Israelite
Samaria. In 722 it was occupied by the Assyrians,
who deported a large part of its population. But its
history did not end here. After many changes of fortune, of which we shall endeavour to give some
account, the city was destined to enter upon a fresh
period of brilliance shortly before the beginning of
the Christian era. 'In the days of Herod the king',
Samaria was one of the proudest cities of Palestine
under Roman domination. It does not appear that
Jesus of Nazareth ever entered it; but it was near
Samaria that his unforgettable meeting with the
Samaritan woman at Jacob's well took place, and
we cannot help recalling, too, the parable of the
Good Samaritan. Nor may we minimize the importance of Samaria from another point of view. When

Christianity began to be a missionary religion, it was in Samaria that messengers from Jerusalem proclaimed the new Gospel. At a later date, tradition assigned to Samaria the site of the tomb of John the Baptist, the Forerunner. From Machaerus where he had been executed, resolute men had carried thither his head, if not his body. It can hardly be contested that, as the scene of so much history, the centre of so many memories, Samaria, next to Jerusalem, can claim to be the most interesting city of Palestine.

I

THE KINGDOM OF ISRAEL

Before the Foundation of Samaria. The death of Solomon about 930 B.C. was the immediate occasion of the break-up of a state which had barely lasted seventy-five years. For its preservation a feeling of national solidarity was needed which could only have been created by several centuries of common national life. Since this was lacking, tribal jealousies broke out afresh, and the old rivalry between North and South once more reared its head. Rehoboam, the son of Solomon, had come up to Shechem, and had attempted to deal with the disaffected elements in a high-handed way.[1] But Jeroboam, who had returned from exile and had been elected king,[2] proved too strong for him, and he was obliged to retreat to Jerusalem. Only two tribes, Judah and Benjamin,[3] adhered to him; the remaining ten enthusiastically acclaimed Jeroboam as king.

This political division which has been called the 'schism' ushered in a period of confusion in Palestine. A united Israel might have served as a centre of cohesion among the various neighbouring states; but

[1] I Kings 12.13.   [2] I Kings 12.20.   [3] I Kings 12.21.

the two divided kingdoms only presented a tempting prey to attackers. Perpetually at enmity, they would be drawn into fatal alliances and incessant fratricidal strife whose disastrous result could only be the destruction and disappearance of both kingdoms.[1]

Jeroboam, the first king of Israel, had seen clearly that religion would constitute the bond of the new state. Links with the past undoubtedly led the king to establish his capital at Shechem:[2] it was the scene of the patriarchal sagas,[3] of the exploits of Joshua and the Judges;[4] near by were the sacred mountains, Gerizim and Ebal.[5] Jerusalem apart, no other city in the north of Palestine possessed so distinguished a past. But Jeroboam went further: by setting up shrines at Bethel and Dan he consecrated his realm to the deity.[6] To the question, which deity? the answer would undoubtedly be, Jahveh, but under the external form of 'the golden calves', that is to say, bulls. Now in Canaanite religion the bull was the theriomorphic symbol of the weather-god, Hadad,[7] and

[1] In 722, Israel, at the hand of the Assyria; in 586, Judah, as the result of the Neo-Babylonian invasion.

[2] I Kings 12.25.

[3] Gen. 12.6 (Abraham), 37.14 (Joseph); Joshua 24.32.

[4] Judg. 9; Josh. 24.

[5] Abel, *Géographie de la Palestine*, I, pp. 360–70. Albright, *The Biblical Period*, p. 31, on the other hand, believes that the new king intended to show his independence of the tribal system, since Shechem was in a Canaanite pocket in the midst of Manasseh.

[6] Dan was at the extreme north of the country, while Bethel was on the southern border.

[7] In the opinion of R. Dussaud, *Les découvertes de Ras Shamra (Ugarit) et l'Ancien Testament*, p. 100, the bull of Bethel represented El,

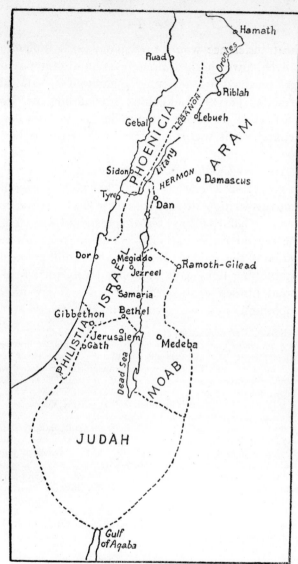

I. Palestine in the Period of the Monarchy

the transference would present no great difficulty. Jahveh, a weather-god himself, would find it easy to take on the attributes of a Canaanite deity, and no orthodox Jahvist would think of confusing the two. This act of Jeroboam came under the severest condemnation: it was stigmatized as 'the sin of Jeroboam.[1]

The choice of Bethel and Dan was due not merely to geographical reasons (fig. 1), but also to the religious associations attaching to these places. While the first site claimed to have been founded by a patriarch,[2] the second could carry its traditions back to the period of the Judges.[3] In spite of his skilful policy of establishing links with tradition, Jeroboam already found himself confronted by open and organized opposition, and was even compelled to abandon

and that of Dan represented Hadad. On the other hand, S. B. Gurewicz maintains that the 'golden calves' were a symbol of national independence, and that it was only later that they became the objects of an idolatrous cult. They were placed at the northern and southern boundaries of the country as guardians of the frontier. The suggestion is new, but somewhat paradoxical. Cf. the bibliography.

[1] 'It was not Jeroboam's intention to change Israel's deity, but in representing the invisible God by the same symbol as Baal-Hadad he debased Jahvism to the level of the surrounding cults and paved the way for the worst kind of syncretism'. R. de Vaux, *Les Livres des Rois*, p. 79, note b. Also the same author's 'Le schisme religieux de Jéroboam I', in *Angelicum*, xx (1943), pp. 77–91.

[2] Gen. 12.8 (Abraham); 28.19 (Jacob). In Jer. 48.13 it is not a place name, but the name of the god Bethel (Cf. *Bible du Centenaire*, note f. to this verse).

[3] Judg. 17–18. R. Dussaud, *Les découvertes de Ras Shamra &c.*, p. 160 is of the opinion that the idol worshipped by the Danites had the form of a young bull.

Shechem and make Penuel his capital,[1] showing that he no longer felt himself safe at Shechem. However his reign continued and was only ended by death after twenty-two years. His son Nadab succeeded him.[2] To all appearance the dynasty seemed securely based, but the appearance was deceptive, for the country was about to experience a succession of revolutions and murders.

Jeroboam's son Nadab actually reigned for only two years.[3] While he was besieging the town of Gibbethon, held by the Philistines, he was assassinated by a certain Baasha, the son of Ahiah, of the tribe of Issachar. The new king immediately slaughtered 'all the house of Jeroboam', and established himself in a new capital, Tirzah,[4] where he reigned for twenty-four years.[5] At his death, his son Elah succeeded him without opposition. Two years later, Zimri, who commanded half his chariots, slew his king while he was drinking in the house of Arza, the steward of the palace.[6]

The army was not unanimous. That part of it which was encamped before Gibbethon,[7] on hearing

---

[1] I Kings 12.25.   [2] I Kings 14.20.   [3] I Kings 15.25.
[4] I Kings 15.33. The site has not been identified with certainty. For the various proposed sites (Talluza, Teiyasir, Tell el-Far'a, el-'Araq), see Abel. *Géographie de la Palestine*, II, p. 485. Père de Vaux, who is now excavating at Far'a, thinks, after much hesitation, that the site may be that of Tirzah. This was the view of W. F. Albright, put forward in 1931 in *JPOS*, XI, p. 241.
[5] I Kings 15.33.   [6] I Kings 16.9–10.
[7] Gibbethon, a town of Philistia, no doubt the modern Tell el-Melath, cf. Abel, *op. cit.*, II, p. 333.

what had happened, proclaimed Omri[1] the commander-in-chief as king. The latter, leaving Gibbethon, marched on Tirzah and besieged the capital. Zimri, seeing himself doomed, set fire to the palace and perished in the flames after a reign of seven days.[2]

This, however, did not end the crisis, for the people were divided. One party adhered to Omri, while the other, about equal in numbers, followed a person named Tibni. From the ordeal of battle Omri emerged triumphant.[3] The way was clear. Samaria was about to enter on the stage of history.

*   *   *

Samaria, the Capital of Israel. Omri and Ahab. The first mention of Samaria in the Old Testament occurs in I Kings 16.24. The notice is remarkably brief. After having stated that Omri reigned twelve years over Israel, six of which were at Tirzah, the annalist continues as follows: 'And he bought the hill Samaria (Heb. Shomeron) of Shemer for two talents of silver; and he built on the hill, and called the name of the city which he built, after the name of Shemer, the

---

[1] Alt regards the name Omri (man of the sheaf) as of Canaanite origin. M. Noth, *Histoire d'Israël*, p. 240, derives it from Arabic. In a Latin inscription from the Lebanon the name Omrius has been found, cf. J. A. Montgomery, 'A Latin Inscription in the Lebanon', in *AASOR*, II-III (1923), pp. 116–18.

[2] I Kings 16.15–18.   [3] I Kings 16.21.

owner of the hill, Samaria' (Heb. Shomeron),[1]
Whether this etymological derivation is correct or
not,[2] it may be admitted that a more appropriate
name could hardly have been chosen for this site,[3]
one of the finest 'watch-towers' in the 'hill-country
of Ephraim'.

Since Shechem, Penuel, and Tirzah had proved
unsatisfactory, Omri, who was not only king of
Israel but also commander-in-chief, was faced with
the problem of finding a site possessing the necessary
qualifications for the capital of the State (fig. II). It
took him six years to come to a decision, but having
reached it he acted at once.[4] Shemer was the owner
of the land. Omri paid him two talents of silver[5] and
set to work to carry out his plans.

It would appear that he did not find it necessary
to clear away any buildings of importance before

---

[1] The LXX reads $\Sigma\epsilon\mu\epsilon\rho\omega\nu$ and $\Sigma\alpha\mu\acute{a}\rho\epsilon\iota\alpha$ (from I Kings 16.28
onwards). The Assyrians knew it under the name Samerina. The
little modern village built close to the ruins is called Sebastiyeh,
corresponding exactly to Sebaste of Herod the Great's time.

[2] Père Abel, *op. cit.*, II, p. 444, raises the question whether the
original name was not Shamir, where the judge named Tola lived
and was buried (Judg. 10.12.)

[3] Shomeron may indeed also mean 'watch-post', see *Bible du
Centenaire*, note on I Kings 16.24. Altitude 443 m. above sea-level.

[4] In a recent monograph, *Der Stadtstaat Samaria* (1954), A. Alt has
argued for the view that the new State had two capitals: Samaria,
the *Canaanite* centre of the kingdom, side by side with Jezreel, the
Israelite centre. The former was the personal property of the dynasty
(viz. that founded by Omri) and could be inherited, while the latter
was based on the charismatic principle of election to the kingship.

[5] I Kings 16.24. About £12,000.

II. Central District of the Kingdom of Israel

erecting his palace. There were no ruins to hinder his progress.[1] What he did lack was time, for he had only six years[2] to make Shomeron into a capital. The

[1] Père Vincent was the first to discover traces of occupation belonging to the end of what Palestinian archaeologists have called the Early Bronze Age (*c.* 2000 B.C.), after which the site was deserted. Cf. *RB*, 1946, pp. 589–90 and n. 2.

[2] I Kings 16.23. According to Albright, *BASOR*, 100 (1945), p. 20, the time must be still further reduced to two years.

biblical tradition contained in the book of Kings is tantalizingly concise. It merely refers us to a lost source, 'the chronicles of the Kings of Israel', but does not fail to pass a severe judgement on this monarch, who sinned worse than his fathers, among his sins being 'the sin of Jeroboam'.[1]

The Bible tells us nothing about the king's successful foreign policy. It is to the Mesha[2] stele that we owe our knowledge of the fact that by his conquest of Moab, Omri controlled Transjordan. It is, furthermore, significant that it was during the reign of the first king of Samaria that Ashurnazirpal (883–859) reached the Phoenician coast and received tribute from its cities.[3] He did not, however, invade the territory of Israel, a testimony, no doubt, to his wholesome respect for that country. It is, at all events, a striking fact that throughout the whole course of their history the only name by which the Assyrians referred to Israel was *Bit-Humri* or *Bit-Humria* (house of Omri), and they spoke of her kings as *mar-Humri* (sons of Omri),[4] even though that dynasty had long since disappeared.

From the first the dynasty had been firmly established, and the dead king's son Ahab succeeded to

[1] An allusion to the cult practices described above, pp. 16–18.

[2] See below p. 33.

[3] Arvad, Gebal (Byblos), Sidon, Tyre. See *Nineveh and the Old Testament*, pp. 31–2.

[4] The irony of this is obvious when we find Shalmaneser styling Jehu (842-815) the son of Omri, whose whole house Jehu had assassinated.

the throne without opposition.[1] He reigned twenty years[2] (869–850), a reign which might have been longer if it had not been cut short by a violent death, this time on the field of battle. During this period the Aramaeans of Damascus and the Israelites of Samaria were in a state of continual war with each other. On one occasion only, at the battle of Qarqar,[3] did they form an alliance to bar the road to the Assyrian advance, but, when once the immediate threat was averted, Ahab and Ben-hadad were again at daggers drawn.

While the whole reign of Omri is recorded and judged in a few lines,[4] the annalist has considered that of Ahab worthy of fuller treatment.[5] Such, indeed, it deserved, for important events, both external and internal, took place during it. According to the judgement of the biblical annalist, this king 'did evil above all that were before him',[6] for he went even beyond Jeroboam. After having married Jezebel,[7] the

[1] I Kings 16.28.

[2] We are here following the chronology of Albright, *loc. cit.* pp. 20–21. The twenty-two years of I Kings 16.29 have accordingly been slightly reduced.

[3] For all this see *Nineveh and the Old Testament*, pp. 33–4, and below p. 4.

[4] I Kings 16.23–28, six verses in all.

[5] I Kings 16.29–34; 17–22. 40.

[6] I Kings 16.30.

[7] Hebrew *'izebel* (cf. our Isabel). This name is made up of *'i* (abbreviation of *'ahi*, 'my brother', or *'abi*, 'my father') and *Zebel* (the name of a Phoenician god). The name means: 'Zebel is my brother' (or 'my father').

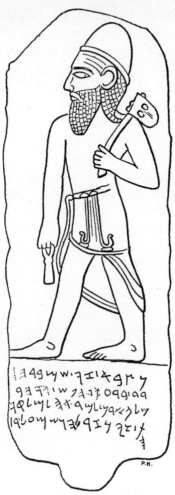

III. Melqart, God of Tyre (from de Vaux, in
Bulletin du Musée de Beyrouth, *III*)

daughter of Ethbaal king of Sidon,[1] he had not only built a temple in Samaria for Melqart, his wife's god[2] (fig. III), but he had also participated in the worship of Melqart, prostrating himself and offering sacrifice to the image of Melqart.[3] Thus the Canaanite cult was not only tolerated, but officially recognized. The adherents of Jahvism could not accept such a situation and opposed it strenuously. The protagonist of the resistance was the prophet Elijah, who was several times obliged to go into hiding[4] to escape the vengeance of the redoubtable queen who was prepared to use drastic means to attain her ends.[5] Her husband would seem to have been unable to refuse her anything.

[1] Ethbaal, 'with Baal', is the Hebrew transcription of the correct form Ittobaal, 'Baal is with him'. There is evidence for an Ittobaal, king of Tyre, about 887–856. The title 'king of the Sidonians' means king of the whole Phoenician coastal strip, of which Sidon and Tyre were the chief cities.

[2] Our knowledge of the pictorial representation of Melqart ('king of the city', or, according to some scholars, 'king of the underworld'), has been recently increased by a stele now in the Aleppo museum, cf. M. Dunand, 'Stèle araméenne dediée à Melqart', in *Bulletin du Musée de Beyrouth*, III (1939), pp. 65–76; VI (1942–3), pp. 41–5; R. de Vaux, *ibid.* V (1941), p. 9; W. F. Albright, in *BASOR*, 87 (1942), pp. 23–39 (with illustration); 90 (1943), pp. 32–4; G. Levi della Vida, *ibid.* 90 (1943), pp. 30–2; R. Dussaud, in *Syria*, XXV (1948), pp. 208–9; A. Herdner, *ibid.* pp. 329–30; A. Jepsen, in *AfO*, XVI (1953), pp. 315–17 (date: shortly before 870 B.C.).

[3] A. Lods, *Israël, des origines au milieu du VIIIe siècle*, p. 489.

[4] By the brook Kerith (I Kings 17.3), at Zarephath on the Phoenician coast (I Kings 17.9), and as far away as Mount Horeb, in the extreme south of Palestine (I Kings 19.8).

[5] As she clearly showed in the matter of Naboth's vineyard (I Kings 21).

This prophetic resistance to the absolute power of the monarch is evidence of a changed attitude among the people. Henceforth a man could threaten the king with death in the name of Jahveh,[1] both for social and for religious reasons.[2] The prophet who dared to do this found himself opposed to the prophets of 'good fortune' who, equally in the name of Jahveh, persistently prophesied of a happy future to come.[3] Such prophets were isolated individuals,[4] nonconformists, uncontaminated by court influence, but it is obvious that they must occasionally have been weary and discouraged,[5] when all seemed lost, and the struggle unavailing against the unrelenting hostility of the court.[6]

[1] The increase of severity may be observed in the oracles of Abijah against the house of Jeroboam (I Kings 14.10), in those of Jehu against that of Baasha (I Kings 16.3–4), and in the bold challenge of Elijah confronting Ahab (I Kings 21.19). But above all the contrast may be seen with the time of Saul, when David could say, 'The Lord forbid that I should put forth mine hand against the Lord's anointed' (I Sam. 26.11).

[2] The seizure of Naboth's vineyard, for example (I Kings 21). This property was not at Samaria, but at Jezreel (cf. I Kings 9.25–6), on the edge of the plain of Esdraelon, where the king had another abode.

[3] In the case of Zedekiah, for instance, who prophesied victory over the Aramaeans, 'in the name of Jahveh', and with the support of his colleagues (I Kings 21.11–12).

[4] Among them was Micaiah (I Kings 22.9,13–28), who is not to be confused with the canonical prophet of that name who lived more than a century later.

[5] Elijah, for instance, who exclaimed: 'It is enough; now, O Lord, take away my life' (I Kings 19.4).

[6] Even if the facts have been dramatized and simplified, as A. Lods insists in *Israël*, p. 488, it is none the less true that Jezebel would never tamely accept any prophetic action.

[27]

Nevertheless, Elijah had won a resounding victory in the historic encounter staged on Mount Carmel. On the one side stood Elijah, representing the cause of Jahveh, on the other the 450 prophets of Baal. It may be recalled that the issue to be decided was

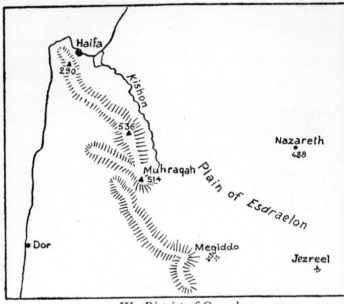

IV. District of Carmel

the termination of a three years' drought by a sacrifice which was to be at the same time a test: the god who should kindle the wood of the sacrifice would be the true God.[1]

---

[1] A. Lods maintains, *op. cit.* p. 490, that it was not a question of knowing who was God in the absolute sense, but who was God *in*

The episode on Carmel is one of the most familiar in the story of the beginnings of prophecy, and has often been studied by expositors, students of the history of religion, and topographers. One tradition has placed the site of the sacrifice (fig. IV) at el-Muhraqah, on the south-east of the range, while another puts it on the north-west, near the modern town of Haifa.[1] In a very original essay,[2] Père de Vaux drew attention to a number of features of the story which seemed to refer definitely to the Baal of Tyre, that is, Melqart,[3] disagreeing with those who would identify the deity of the mountain, either with a local Baal,[4] or with the Syrian Baalshamim, the lord of heaven.[5]

The recent publication of a fragment of sculpture with a Greek inscription, found in a monastery on

---

Israel. On the other hand, R. de Vaux, in *Les Livres des Rois*, p. 101, thinks that it was 'the monotheistic belief' which was 'the vital issue in this test'. This seems doubtful, for this stage had not yet been reached in the religious development of Israel.

[1] Abel, *Géographie de la Palestine*, I, pp. 351-2, states that the water in question might have been drawn, on the first assumption, at Bir-el-Mansura, about twelve minutes' climb.

[2] R. de Vaux, 'Les prophètes de Baal sur le Mont Carmel', in the *Bulletin du musée de Beyrouth*, V (1941), pp. 7-20.

[3] R. Dussaud, 'Melqart', in *Syria*, XXV (1948), pp. 205-30; W. F. Albright, *Archaeology and the Religion of Israel*, pp. 80, 196; H. Seyrig, 'Héraclès, Melkart et Nergal', in *Syria*, XXIV (1944-5), pp. 69-71.

[4] A. Alt, 'Das Gottesurteil auf dem Karmel,' in *Festschrift Georg Beer* (1935), pp. 1-18, reprinted in *Kleine Schriften zur Geschichte des Volkes Israel*, II (1953), pp. 135-49. M. Noth, *Histoire d'Israël*, p. 252, n. 5, has given his support to this view.

[5] O. Eissfeldt, 'Ba'alshamêm und Jahwe,' in *ZATW*, 1939, pp. 1-31.

Mount Carmel,[1] has re-opened the question, and in various important articles scholars have sought, with the help of this late inscription (second century A.D.), to reach some certainty concerning an event which had happened more than a thousand years earlier.[2] The sites, however, remain the same, and the point at issue is whether the vanquished god on this historic occasion,[3] when Jahveh hearkened to the voice of Elijah and sent down fire[4] to consume the sacrifice, thus vindicating his unquestionable superiority, was Melqart, Baalshamim, or Hadad.

Ahab, however, was more concerned with the threat to his northern frontier than with the extermination of the prophets of Baal.[5] The enemy, consisting of the Aramaeans of Damascus, had invaded in

[1] M. Avi-Yonah, 'Mount Carmel and the God of Baalbek', in *Israel Exploration Journal*, II, 2 (1952), pp. 118–24. The object in question is a votive foot, no doubt of a deity, dedicated to the Heliopolitan Zeus (god of) Carmel (by) Gaius Julius Eutychas, citizen of Caesarea.

[2] O. Eissfeldt, *Der Gott Karmel* (1953); K. Galling, 'Der Gott Karmel und die Achtung der fremden Götter', in *Festschrift Alt* (1953), pp. 105–25.

[3] It is well illustrated by a fine stained glass window in the church of St John (Sint Janskerk) of Gouda (Netherlands).

[4] Lightning, according to the commentators. A. Lucas, in *PEQ*, Jan.–April 1945, discussed the miracle on Carmel in the light of a passage in II Mac. 1.19–22, where it is a question of 'thick water' poured on an altar and catching fire by the sun's rays. Hence the water mentioned in I Kings 18.35 might have been some inflammable substance, such as methane or some similar product of distillation. This view is open to the objection that at the time of the sacrifice (v. 36) it was already late in the afternoon, when the sun's rays would have lost much of their power.   [5] I Kings 18.40.

force, and had even succeeded in besieging Samaria.[1]
This was the only occasion during his reign on which
the country was invaded. The subsequent actions
were fought on the frontier, in Transjordan. Ahab
won the battle of Apheq,[2] and it was after the peace
which followed that Ahab, with his late adversary,
and with the king of Hamath, set out to bar the way
to the Assyrian advance under Shalmaneser III.
(858–824 B.C.).

In the engagement which took place at Qarqar
neither side could claim the victory.[3] Ahab had
quickly dropped out of the alliance, having no intention of giving even temporary assistance to his neighbour, against whom we find him shortly after at war.
In the battle before Ramoth-Gilead[4] the king of
Israel was fatally wounded in his chariot. The episode[5] is related with an economy of effect which

---

[1] I Kings 20.1–21. The league consisted of 'thirty-two kings'.

[2] I Kings 20.26. The modern Fiq, east of the Lake of Tiberias and
south of the Gaulan plateau. The numbers are evidently exaggerated,
as are the losses sustained by the Damascenes: 100,000 slain in a
single day (I Kings 20.29), and 27,000 buried under the city wall
(v. 30)!

[3] The biblical annalist has entirely ignored these events. See
Nineveh and the Old Testament, p. 33.

[4] The site has not been identified with complete certainty. Husn
Ajlun has been suggested, about 16 miles south-west of Deraah, and
still in Transjordan. The name has no doubt been preserved in the
modern Ramethah. See Abel, *op. cit.* II, pp. 430–1, who accepts
Dalman's theory. Recently N. Glueck has suggested as a site for
Ramoth-Gilead, Tell Ramith, which is about five miles south of
Ramethah (*BASOR*, 92 (1943), p. 12; *The River Jordan*, p. 170).

[5] I Kings 22.29–38.

enhances its vividness. Ahab withdraws from the
fight, wounded by an arrow, but did not leave the
field. Bleeding from his wound, he remained standing in his chariot, so that he might be seen by the
enemy as well as by his soldiers. In the evening he
collapsed as the result of the haemorrhage from his
unstanched wound. A general flight ensued. They
brought back the corpse of the king to Samaria, and
washed the chariot in the pool.[1]

As in the case of his father Omri, the biblical
annalists refer us vainly to the book of the Chronicles
of the Kings of Israel, a source which, as we have
already said, has been lost. The only detailed information refers to 'the ivory house' which the king had
built,[2] and the record of his reign closes with the
stereotyped formula, 'and Ahab slept with his
fathers.'[3]

*   *   *

The End of the House of Ahab. Although it raised no
question of the succession, since Ahaziah[4] followed
his father without opposition, the death of Ahab left
the state facing serious external dangers. Foreign
enemies had diagnosed the situation correctly; the

---

[1] I Kings 22.38.

[2] Indication will be given further on of the way in which archaeology has, nevertheless, thrown light on all these details.

[3] The royal tombs of Israel have not yet been excavated.

[4] This theophorous name compounded with Jahveh (there is
Ahaziah or Ahaziahu), shows clearly that Ahab had not completely
forsaken the national God, cf. A. Lods, *op. cit.*, p. 488.

1. *The Hill of Samaria*

2. *The Infant Horus*   3. *The God Ra offering the figurine of M*

4. *The God Hah*

Ivories from the Royal Palaces

strong man was gone, and the opportunity must be seized. Moab was the first to take action,[1] by revolting against Israel which, since the time of Omri, had occupied part of its territory, the district of Medeba. Our knowledge of these events, unmentioned in the Bible, is derived from the detailed information contained in the Mesha stele.[2] Ahaziah had no opportunity of retaliation since he died as the result of a fall.[3] The task devolved upon his brother Joram[4] (849–842), who attempted[5] to carry it out, but without success: Mesha prevailed, and with the help of his god Chemosh he recovered his territory.

This first reverse was the prelude to more serious disasters, this time from the Aramaean arms. It is almost impossible to arrange the recorded events[6] in

---

[1] II Kings 1.1; 3.5.

[2] R. Dussaud, *Les monuments palestiniens et judaïques*, pp. 4–20; A. Parrot, *Le Département des Antiquités orientales*, p. 14, Plate 1. This monument will be discussed in detail in a forthcoming study.

[3] II Kings 1.2, 17. The king fell from a lofty room in his palace, through 'the lattice of the window'. Severely injured, he sent without delay to consult Baal-Zebub, the god of Ekron. It is possible that the real name of this deity was not Baal-Zebub (lord of flies), but Baal-Zebul (= Aliyan-Baal of Ras Shamra), mentioned in the New Testament, Matt. 10.25; Luke 11.18.

[4] This second son of Ahab also bore a theophorous name, Joram, in honour of Jahveh. Cf. above p. 32, n. 4.

[5] II Kings 3.7. On this campaign Joram's allies were Jehoshaphat, king of Judah, and the 'king' of Edom (v. 9), whose territory they were making use of. For the title 'king' designating the last named, cf. *Bible du Centenaire*, note on II Kings 3.9.

[6] All the commentators are agreed on this point, as are also A. Lods, *Bible du Centenaire*, II, pp. 248–9, and R. de Vaux, *Les Livres des Rois*, p. 145, note c.

any chronological order; they are often connected with the activity of a new prophet, Elisha, the disciple and successor of Elijah. Samaria was besieged, but, thanks to its situation and its defences,[1] it again avoided capture, and the struggle was continued on the frontiers, and, as in the time of Ahab, over Ramoth-Gilead which the army of Hazael, king of Aram, was besieging in the attempt to recover it from Joram. He, like his father, exposed himself to the dangers of battle, and, like his father, was wounded and carried off to Jezreel in order that he might convalesce there. At this point Jehu, an officer in the Israelite army, makes his appearance.

*   *   *

Jehu's Coup d'Etat. Jehu's sudden appearance is linked up with prophetic activity. We are to see a man of God, to wit Elisha, placing on the throne a hitherto unknown claimant. There are few more vivid passages in the history of Israel than those contained in these two chapters of the second book of Kings.[2] Rarely can an annalist have painted the narrative of a *coup d'état* in more realistic colours, or conveyed more clearly the passions and sanguinary violence there displayed.

It had been necessary for Joram, wounded at Ramoth-Gilead (fig. V), as we have said, to retire to

---

[1] For all this cf. below p. 58.   [2] II Kings 9–10.

Jezreel to recuperate. There his nephew[1] Ahaziah, king of Judah, came to visit him, no doubt to consult with his uncle, whose ally he was, concerning the conduct of the war. This was the moment which Elisha chose for swift and decisive action. He sent one of his disciples to Ramoth on an urgent mission: he was ordered to anoint Jehu, an army officer, as king of Israel.[2] Everything was carried out according to plan, and the army rallied immediately round the new king.

But first it was necessary to dispose of the old king, and this task Jehu took upon himself. Having given orders that no one was to leave Ramoth, lest the news of what had happened should reach Jezreel before he could get there, he mounted his chariot and left Ramoth, driving so furiously that his train found it difficult to keep up with him. As his small company drew near to Jezreel, the sentinel watching the approaches to the city gave warning of its arrival. The king, anxious to know the meaning of this movement, sent out a horseman to meet the advancing strangers.[3] But the horseman did not return. The

[1] The mother of Ahaziah was actually Athaliah, the daughter of Ahab and Jezebel. She had married Joram, king of Judah. See the chronological table on p. 130.

[2] It may be conceded that Elisha and Jehu were in agreement over the carrying out of the affair.

[3] The messenger, who was to take back the news, asks, 'Is all well?' In the royal archives of Mari, correspondents writing to king Zimri-Lim were already using the same formula about a thousand years before: 'It is well with the palace of Mari, and the city of Mari.'

same thing happened to a second messenger. In his impatience the king ordered his chariot to be harnessed and, accompanied by his visitor, Ahaziah, set out to meet Jehu whom the sentinel had recognized by his furious driving. The two companies met

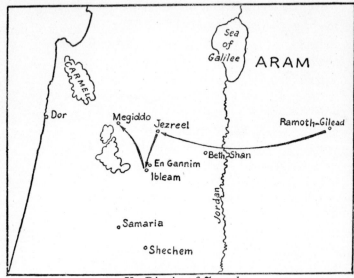

V. District of Jezreel

and things happened swiftly. Jehu drew his bow and pierced the heart of Joram with an arrow. The dead king's body was thrown down onto the floor of the chariot.[1] Ahaziah, king of Judah, who was in his own

[1] This duty was performed by Bidqar, the 'third' man in the chariot (II Kings 9.25). As in the Assyrian chariots, the king was accompanied by a driver and an assistant, cf. *Nineveh and the Old Testament*, p. 37, fig. VIII.

chariot, attempted flight, but he was overtaken[1] and wounded. He managed to reach Megiddo[2] where he died. Jehu, having wiped out his two most important rivals, reached Jezreel, where he found his third victim, Ahab's wife, Jezebel, awaiting him and death with courage and a certain panache.[3] She was thrown down from a window, and her broken corpse was devoured by dogs.[4] A double curse was wreaked upon her: she was eaten by unclean beasts, and her body received no burial.

Jehu, however, although master of Jezreel, had not yet won Samaria. The officials and nobles of the capital, panic-stricken, immediately demonstrated their subservience by sending to him in baskets the heads of the 'seventy sons of Ahab'. Jehu ordered

[1] Ahaziah had fled by the road of 'the garden house', which may be identified with En-Gannim ('the fountain of the gardens'), the modern Jenin. By getting into the hilly country he stood a better chance of escaping and was also on the way to Jerusalem. However, he was overtaken near Ibleam (II Kings 9.27), identified with Tell Belama, about one mile south of Jenin. Cf. Abel, *op. cit.*, II, p. 357.

[2] After reaching Megiddo, the royal chariot must have turned back, for this town is about 14 miles to the north-west, on the edge of the plain of Jezreel. It is impossible to explain the reason for his taking this direction, and the text may be corrupt.

[3] The old queen had painted and bedizened herself (II Kings 9.30), no doubt 'to repair the irreparable wreck of years', but also to receive her adversary. She receives him, not with a plea for mercy, but with a bitter taunt.

[4] In her dream, in Racine's play, Athaliah sees 'this horrible mass of shattered flesh and bones, mud-soiled and bloody morsels of flesh and grisly limbs, over which the greedy dogs are snarling' (Act II, Scene V).

them to be displayed[1] in two heaps at the gate of
Jezreel. The time was ripe for an official entry into
Samaria. On his way thither he was met by forty-
two members of the royal family of Judah, who, leaving Jerusalem in ignorance of the events which had
taken place, had come to visit their relations in
Israel. Jehu took the precaution of having them
stopped and executed, and seems to have disposed of
their bodies by having them thrown into a cistern.[2]

But the blood-bath was not yet complete. Samaria
underwent a drastic purge. All who were left of the
house of Ahab were slain, and in order to consum-
mate the extirpation of the worshippers of Baal, Jehu
proclaimed a solemn assembly in which he pretended
to take part officially. All those who attended were
ruthlessly butchered, and the *coup d'état* was complete.[3]
Two things, however, surprise us: why Elisha, who
was the instigator of the revolt,[4] was not associated

[1] The heaps of severed heads were in keeping with the outlook of
the age. They are frequently depicted on Assyrian reliefs, cf. *Nineveh
and the Old Testament*, p. 67, fig. XV. In the palace of Khorsabad, the
base of the throne of Sargon, the future conqueror of Samaria, was
decorated with a similar scene.

[2] This may be inferred from the text (II Kings 10.14). Excavations
have frequently disclosed cisterns which have been turned into
charnel-houses. Cf. Jer. 41.9.

[3] According to A. Alt, *Der Stadtstaat Samaria*, p. 40, the monarchy
continued to be dynastic, but lost the dual character which it had
possessed since the time of Omri. Samaria became an Israelite city,
and the only capital of Israel.

[4] Jonadab, the Rechabite, whom we find associated with Jehu on
more than one occasion (II Kings 10.15, 23) is of only secondary importance in comparison with the prophet.

with Jehu in its accomplishment, and why Jehu did not seize Jerusalem at the moment when it was without a king, Ahaziah having disappeared.[1] Be that as it may, Israel had a new master. As often happens in such cases the difficulties remained, and the external peril was more threatening than ever. So far as the religious situation was concerned, the cult of the Tyrian Baal seemed to be definitely and permanently disposed of, but orthodox Jahvism had not been re-established, and Jehu still maintained at Dan and Bethel the worship of 'the golden calves' of the first king of Israel.[2]

*   *   *

The Dynasty of Jehu. Jehu's reign lasted for twenty-eight years (842–815). Detailed as is the account which the biblical annalists have given us of the *coup d'état*, their narrative of the subsequent events is equally concise. To the storm succeeded a calm in internal affairs, but abroad the horizon was lowering. The Assyrian menace revived, and Jehu, who had no cause to mourn the fate of Damascus,[3] sent tribute

---

[1] It is true that Athaliah was still at Jerusalem, and would not surrender without a struggle.   [2] II Kings 10.29.

[3] Merely for sentimental reasons, since political reasons pointed to an alliance with Aram. The wholesale executions which accompanied Jehu's seizure of power had deprived him of all possible friends and allies. He could no longer look for help either to Phoenicia, or to Judah. It should be remarked that these drastic measures had not met with universal approval. The prophet Hosea explicitly condemns them (1.4), 'I will avenge the blood of Jezreel upon the house of Jehu'.

to Shalmaneser III[1] (fig. VI) in order to avoid an even worse fate. When the soldiers of the king of Assyria returned home, the king of Damascus, Hazael, whose name occurs on the ivories found at Arslan Tash (fig. VII)[2] and whose figure may perhaps be

VI. The Tribute of Jehu (Obelisk of Shalmaneser)

[1] The Bible does not record this act of submission, but the Assyrian king published it on his black obelisk, now in the British Museum. For details see *Nineveh and the Old Testament*, p. 35 and Plate 3. The most recent study of the monument is by Ernst Michel, 'Die Assur-Texte Salmanassars III (858–824)' in *Die Welt des Orients*, 1955, pp. 137–9.

[2] Thureau-Dangin, *Arslan Tash*, pp. 135–6, fig. 49. It is an interesting fact that Jehu and Hazael were both usurpers. The narrative of II Kings 8.15 is in complete agreement with all that we learn from Assyrian sources. They relate that Hazael, 'the son of nobody', succeeded to the throne of Damascus in the place of Hadad-ezer who was slain (Gressmann, *AOT*[2], p. 344; *ANET*, p. 280. Inscription on the statue of Shalmaneser, found at Ashur.)

seen on the same ivories (fig. VIII),[1] immediately
retaliated on his neighbour and finally settled the
vexed question of the disputed territory. He took
possession of all the Israelite territory in Transjordan,[2]

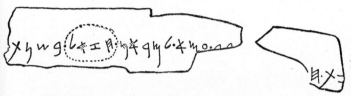

*VII. Ivory inscribed with the name of Hazael (from
Thureau-Dangin, Arslan Tash p. 135)*

including the region of Gilead and the famous fortress
of Ramoth, over which so many previous battles had
been fought. Jehu could only submit to this loss of
territory without attempting to recover it.[3] On his

---

[1] Those who reject this identification should be prepared to offer
some alternative. Thureau-Dangin, *op. cit.* p. 111, says 'It is very
probable that this figure represents a Syrian prince, of whom it may
well be a portrait.'

[2] II Kings 10.32–3; Amos 1.3–4.

[3] Racine has put words into the mouth of Athaliah which suggest
that the author had an accurate knowledge of the historical situation
in which his characters are depicted as taking part: 'Jehu, proud
Jehu, trembles in Samaria. Harassed on every side by the powerful
neighbour whom I have stirred up against him, he is obliged to leave
me to rule these regions in peace.' (Act II, Scene V.) In the 'neighbour' it is easy to recognize Hazael, and it is quite possible that
Athaliah, the granddaughter of the king of Tyre, may have
intrigued with the king of Damascus against their common enemy.

*VIII. Ivory from Arslan Tash: Hazael (?),
King of Damascus (from Thureau-Dangin, op.
cit. Pl. XXXIII, 43*

death his son Jehoahaz[1] succeeded to the throne and reigned for sixteen years (815–801)[2] but all we know of the period is that it witnessed a fresh diminution of Israelite power, still at the hand of Damascus. First Hazael, and then his son Ben-hadad,[3] made great inroads into Palestine. In doing this they skirted the State of Israel on the west, and pushed so far south as to threaten Jerusalem.[4] The new king of Judah, the young Joash, whom the priest Jehoida had rescued from the clutches of Athaliah,[5] bought off his adversary by hurriedly delivering over to him all the gold stored up in the treasuries of the Temple

[1] II Kings 10.35; 13.1. The Vulgate renders the name as Joachaz. In Hebrew it is Jeho'ahaz.

[2] Seventeen years, according to II Kings 13.1.

[3] II Kings 13.3. The reference is to Ben-hadad III, to be distinguished from two other kings of the same name who reigned in Damascus, and who are mentioned respectively in I Kings 15.18 (in the time of Baasha), and I Kings 20.1 (in the time of Ahab). This Ben-Hadad was known to the Assyrians under the name of Adad-idri. Not all scholars admit that there were three kings of Damascus named Ben-Hadad. A. Dupont-Sommer, *Les Araméens*, pp. 33–5, 47, is positive that there were three. On the other hand, W. F. Albright, *BASOR*, 87, pp. 27–8, believes that there were only two. M. Noth, *Histoire d'Israël*, p. 255, is also doubtful on the point. Dhorme in *RB*, 1910, p. 72, distinguishes three Ben-Hadads, but nevertheless styles the son of Hazael Ben-Hadad II.

[4] The Philistine town of Gath had been captured by them (II Kings 12.17).

[5] This is the subject of Racine's play, produced at the Comédie Française in April 1955, with bold and clever scenery by Carzou. The artist, who probably drew his information from Perrot and Chipiez, has fallen into certain anachronisms: he has prominently featured a candlestick with seven branches. Unfortunately this type of candlestick was not in existence in Athaliah's time, and was not set up in the Temple until three hundred years later.

and the palace.[1] Jehoahaz, king of Israel, no doubt
felt that the misfortunes of his neighbour were fortun-
ate for him, for his sorely reduced forces[2] would have
been absurdly outnumbered at their first encounter.

However, a time came when Israel in her turn
profited by the disasters which befell Damascus at
the hands of Assyria. Adadnirari III (809–782) returned and overcame a league of the Syrian kings.[3]
Israel and Judah seized the opportunity to settle
accounts between them. Joash of Israel (801–786)
attacked and defeated Amaziah of Judah (800–783)[4]:
Jerusalem was captured, her walls destroyed, and
she was forced to pay tribute.[5] Moreover, the king of
Israel recovered from Aram some of the cities which
his father had been obliged to surrender.[6] Hence,
at his death, the Northern Kingdom had recovered
its lost ground, a process which was successfully continued by Jeroboam II.

Jeroboam II (786–746). There can be no doubt that

---

[1] II Kings 12.18.

[2] Certainly, there were ten thousand foot-soldiers, but only fifty
horsemen and ten chariots (II Kings 13.7), whereas Ahab could pro-
duce two thousand at the battle of Qarqar.

[3] Hazael was the moving spirit (on the stele of Saba‘a, where
Adadnirari III records his campaign, the king of Damascus is called
'Mari', cf. de Vaux, in *RB*, 1934, p. 516). Assyrian text in *ANET*,
p. 282.

[4] It is extremely difficult to determine the chronology because of
the conflicting data. The duration of the reign given as twenty-nine
years in II Kings 14.2, is usually reduced to eighteen (cf. Albright
in *BASOR*, 100 (1945), p. 21).

[5] II Kings 14.12–14.   [6] II Kings 13.25.

the new king was one of the greatest of the kings of
Israel. No king enjoyed a longer reign (forty-one
years[1]), and under no other king did the country
enjoy a greater prosperity. However, the biblical
annalist is strangely reticent about him,[2] for the
reason that Jeroboam 'had done evil in the sight of
the Lord'. It could not be denied, however, that the
frontiers had been restored, 'from the entering in of
Hamath' on the north, to 'the sea of the Arabah' on
the south,[3] and this had been the work of Jeroboam.
The mere fact is stated, but without a word of praise;
and the annalist prefers to refer the reader to 'the book
of the Chronicles of the Kings of Israel', not however,
without mentioning the valour of the monarch.[4]

The prophet Amos issued his challenge to Jeroboam. In the shrine of Bethel itself, 'in the midst of
the house of Israel', the shepherd of Judaean Tekoa
boldly predicted the death of the king and the cap-
tivity of his people.[5] After pronouncing judgement
on Damascus, Gaza, Tyre, Edom, Ammon, Moab,

[1] II Kings 14.25.
[2] Only six verses for a reign of forty-one years.
[3] II Kings 14.25. Although it is easy to identify the southern
border (which is the Dead Sea), the northern boundary is more difficult to determine. It is doubtful whether it extended as far as the
entrance to the plain through which the Orontes runs, watering
Hamath, or as far as the plain of Beqah, where there is a site called
Lebuah, representing the biblical *lebo' Hamath*. It is not safe to go
beyond the district of Hermon, in the neighbourhood of Mergayun.
Verse 28, which ascribes to Jeroboam the conquest of Damascus and
Hamath is corrupt, and should be discarded. Neither Israel nor
Judah ever possessed either of these cities.
[4] II Kings 14.28.   [5] Amos 8.11.

and Judah, Amos fulminated more directly and at greater length against Israel, her king, and her nobles, charging them with sins committed 'on the hill of Samaria', surrounded by the luxury of their houses of ivory or of ebony.[1] It would appear that the prophets were not unanimous in their condemnation of the king, and that some of them supported him and encouraged him in his policy.[2] He therefore continued to pursue it, and its success is explained by the length of his reign. However, it would be unjust not to emphasize the personal qualities of a king who deserved the good fortune which he enjoyed.

* * *

The Decline and Fall of Israel (746—721 B.C.). In a quarter of a century Israel's recovery came to an end. After the death of Jeroboam II, his son Zechariah only reigned for six months,[3] being assassinated by the usurper Shallum.[4] A month later he too was eliminated by Menahem[5] who probably reigned eight years.[6] This king was compelled to pay a heavy tribute to Tiglathpileser III (745-727)[7] (fig. IX), to-

---

[1] Amos 3.15. We shall see later how much light archaeology has thrown on all these details. In this chapter we have merely outlined the historical background of the city.

[2] Among them should be mentioned Jonah, the son of Amittai, from the Galilean village of Gath-hepher, the modern Mekhed (? Khirbet ezzurra'), 2½ miles north of Nazareth (cf. II Kings 14.25).

[3] II Kigs 15.8.   [4] II Kings 15.10, 13.   [5] II Kings 15.14.

[6] Further chronological difficulties occur here, cf. Albright, *BASOR*, 100, p. 21. Père de Vaux, *op. cit.*, p. 231, only allows six years, instead of the ten given in II Kings 15.17.

[7] II Kings 15.20.

IX. *Tiglathpileser III (from a Relief in the Leyden Museum)*

gether with several other kings, among whom were those of Damascus, Byblos, and Tyre.[1]

The situation steadily deteriorated, nor were the kings who rapidly succeeded one another at Samaria likely to remedy it. Internal disorder,[2] which invariably accompanies the recurrence of external danger, reared its head for the last time: Pekahiah, the son of Menahem, was assassinated by his commander-in-chief Pekah.[3] The army, having regained control, attempted to confront and ward off the one serious threat, namely that from Nineveh. Forgetting all the ancient grievances, Pekah allied himself with Rezin (750–732), the king of Damascus.[4] It was an unfortunate choice, for doom had come upon Aram: the city was taken and all the fortresses of the country destroyed. Rezin was executed.[5]

This catastrophe foreshadowed the coming fate of Israel. For the present she lost her northern and western territory,[6] which became, under Assyrian governors, the Assyrian provinces of Magidu (Megid-

[1] Cf. *Nineveh and the Old Testament*, p. 40.

[2] R. Gordis (*Hebrew Union College Annual*, XXV, 1954), believes that the experience of Hosea, contained in Chapters 1–3 of his book, may be explained by the chaotic condition of the kingdom of Israel about 740 B.C.   [3] II Kings 15.25.

[4] These are 'the two tails of smoking firebrands' in Isa. 7.2, Pekah and Rezin, who attacked Jerusalem in order to punish Ahaz, king of Judah, for his refusal to join the league against the Assyrians.

[5] In *ANET*, p. 283, 592 towns are mentioned, scattered over the sixteen districts of the kingdom. Cf. II Kings 16.9. Unger, in *Archaeology and the Old Testament*, p. 258, following E. Schrader, cites a tablet of Tiglathpileser, read by Rawlinson, which has since disappeared, and which recorded the death of Rezin.   [6] II Kings 15.29.

...ories from the Royal Palaces:

5. *The Egyptian Goddesses Isis and Nepthys*

33·2572

6. *The Winged Sphinx*

7. *The West Gate of the City*

do), Du'ru (Dor, on the Mediterranean coast), and Gal'aza (Gilead, Israelite Transjordan).[1] The population, at least the ruling classes, were deported.

These disasters had an immediate repercussion on internal affairs: Pekah was assassinated and Hoshea, undoubtedly with Assyrian support, became king.[2]

The new king showed himself sufficiently subservient, feeling that tribute was a small price to pay for a throne. This state of affairs lasted until Hoshea was discovered to be intriguing to throw off the Assyrian yoke with the help of Egypt,[3] and was immediately arrested. To avoid any further attempts at revolt, the Assyrian king, at that time Shalmaneser V (726–722) laid siege to Samaria.[4] The city held out for three years, a sufficient testimony to its resources. They were, nevertheless, inadequate to withstand opponents better equipped, and more experienced in siege warfare. In the beginning of 721 the capital fell, and Sargon II (722–705) (fig. X), who had succeeded Shalmaneser on the throne of Nineveh, celebrated his victory with a magnificence which was equal to its importance in his estimation. Below we give the

[1] On these details see Forrer, *Die Provinzeinteilung des assyrichen Reiches*, pp. 59, 69; Alt, 'Das System der assyrichen Provinzen' in *Kleine Schriften*, II, pp. 195–205; Dhorme, in *RB*, 1910, p. 197.

[2] II Kings 15.30. Tiglathpileser says definitely that he placed Hoshea (*A-u-si'*) on the throne of Israel (bit-Humria = the house of Omri).

[3] O. Eissfeldt has put forward the attractive theory that Ps. 29 was composed between 732 and 722 B.C., that is, between the revolt of Hoshea and his capture by the Assyrians (cf. *Geschichte und Altes Testament*, pp. 65–78). [4] II Kings 17.5.

X. Sargon II (from a Relief in Turin, Weidner, in AfO, XI; p. 133)

record, recently discovered in the excavation of Nim-rud,[1] given in parallel columns with the biblical account of the same event:

PRISM OF SARGON	II KINGS 17.5–6
The man of Samaria and a king[2] who was hostile to me, had joined together to refuse homage and tribute to me, and came out to fight with me; by the help of the great gods, my lords, I overthrew them: I captured from them 27,280 persons[3] with their chariots, their gods in whom they trusted,[4] and took as my royal share of the booty 200 chariots. I gave orders that the rest should be settled in the midst of Assyria.[5]	Then the king of Assyria came up throughout all the land, and went up to Samaria, and besieged it three years. In the ninth year of Hoshea, the king of Assyria took Samaria, and carried Israel away unto Assyria, and placed them in Halah, and on the banks of the Habor,[6] on the river of Gozan,[7] and in the cities of the Medes.[8]

[1] Several clay prisms bearing the name of Sargon were discovered by M. E. Mallowan during his excavations at Nimrud in 1952 and 1953. They were published by C. J. Gadd in *Iraq*, XVI (1954), pp. 173–201.

[2] Or Ilu-bi'di of Hamath, or Sib'e of Egypt.

[3] Other texts give 27,290 captives.

[4] This remark is an explicit allusion to the polytheism prevalent in Israel, as Gadd points out, *loc. cit.*, p. 181. But it may be asked whether Sargon was well-informed on this matter.

[5] A deportation lacking the details given in the biblical passage.

[6] A left bank tributary of the Euphrates.

[7] The district of Harran, hence in Upper Mesopotamia.

[8] The campaign of Sargon against Media took place before 714 B.C. Corridor X of the palace of Khorsabad was lined throughout its length with reliefs recording the tribute paid to the king by the envoys of the thirty-four conquered districts. Several of these sculptures are in the Louvre.

The two versions supplement each other exactly and give us the main facts. The capital was captured and denuded by measures suited to the purpose. The essential population of the nation was deported and replaced by alien elements taken from other conquered countries. In the literal meaning of the term they were 'displaced persons'. This is a euphemistic description of the barbarous measures considered necessary by the victors. They had subjugated a fresh victim, and the kingdom of Israel had ceased to exist. Exactly two centuries after its founding it had been wiped off the map. Thanks to archaeological researches we are now better able to estimate how much had disappeared.

II

ISRAELITE SAMARIA IN THE LIGHT OF ARCHAEOLOGY

THE site of Samaria has been the scene of two periods of excavation; first from 1908 to 1910, and then from 1931 to 1935. The first campaign was carried out under the auspices of the American University of Harvard; the second was under the direction of J. W. Crowfoot. For three seasons he conducted a Joint Expedition composed of Harvard University, the Hebrew University of Jerusalem, the Palestine Exploration Fund, the British Academy, and the British School of Archaeology in Jerusalem. The fourth season's excavation was carried out by an English expedition alone.

The excavation of this site presented special difficulties, not because of modern buildings, but because of the gardens and olive plantations, which compelled the archaeologists to proceed by the discontinuous method of trenching in the free areas,[1] rendering the accurate recording of results a matter of no small difficulty. These obstacles account for

---

[1] What J. W. Crowfoot has called 'the strip system'.

some uncertainty in the dating of finds, and for the fact that many problems remain unsolved. The excavators cannot be blamed for this state of affairs, least of all Crowfoot's expedition, whose work deserves all praise and whose results enabled certain corrections to be made in the conclusions of Harvard University.[1]

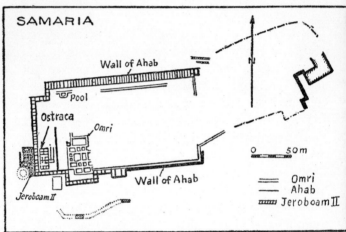

XI. Israelite Samaria (from K. Galling, Biblisches Reallexikon, *col. 441)*

The task of recording the stratigraphy of the site devolved upon Miss Kenyon. She established sixteen periods, seven of which covered the Israelite occupa-

[1] G. A. Reisner, C. S. Fisher and D. G. Lyon, *Harvard Excavations at Samaria* (1908–10), cited as *HES*; J. W. Crowfoot, Kathleen M. Kenyon and E. L. Sukenik, *The Buildings at Samaria*; J. W. Crowfoot and Grace M. Crowfoot, *Early Ivories from Samaria.*

tion of Samaria, which is our present concern. J. W. Crowfoot has assigned them as follows: I–II, the period of Omri and Ahab; III, the period of Jehu; IV–VI, the period of Jeroboam and the eighth century b.c.; VII, the period covering the fall of Samaria (721 b.c.).[1] The delimitation of the periods is no easy matter; for example, it was extremely difficult to determine with exactitude what should be assigned to Omri and what to Ahab, since a maximum of twenty-eight years covers all the activities of these two kings at Samaria.[2] The same uncertainty appears in the attempt to date certain architectural features, when the choice may lie between Ahab and Jeroboam II who are separated by an interval of only sixty years.[3]

When Omri, who was a soldier, chose the hill of Samaria (Plate I) as the site of his capital, he had to keep in mind, not only the building of a palace, but also the construction of fortifications (fig. XI). It is certain that there were from the first two boundary walls: a splendidly built *interior* wall, at least 1½ metres in thickness, and an *external* wall, of the case-

[1] Crowfoot, *The Buildings at Samaria*, p. 8.

[2] Omri (six years), Ahab (twenty-two years) according to I Kings 16.23 and 29. We have seen above (p. 22) that these durations must be reduced by four years.

[3] Not to mention various other important alterations, since certain round towers, formerly attributed by the Harvard archaeologists to the period of Jeroboam II, are at the earliest of Hellenistic date, lowering the date by half a millenium! For these monuments see below p. 99.

mate type, 10 metres in breadth, and flanked at
intervals by towers and bastions which do not seem
to have been closely connected with the wall. The
external wall was built into the rock (fig. XII) which
was specially excavated to receive the masonry of the
wall. Two styles of construction were here apparent:
the one rough and uneven; the other composed of
carefully hewn blocks, regularly laid (fig. XIII).[1]

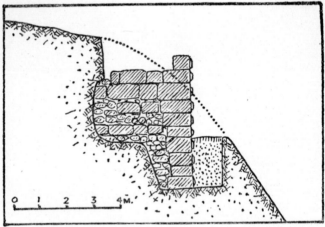

XII. Part of the Wall (from Syria, *1925, p. 324)*

Traces of timber[2] bonding courses were found in this
masonry of hewn stone, which was finished off, per-

[1] The first is now assigned to Omri, the second to Ahab, which
seems the logical conclusion.

[2] An architectural device employed in the Temple at Jerusalem
(I Kings 7.12), and observed in many excavational sites (see *The
Temple of Jerusalem*, p. 41).

haps, in the upper courses, with unbaked bricks.[1]

Side by side with this admirable construction and finished masonry, another architectural feature appeared, namely, pillars crowned with capitals of the

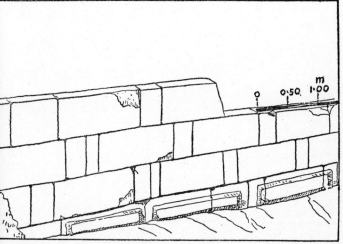

XIII. Israelite Wall (from Crowfoot, The Buildings at Samaria, *Pl. XIII)*

type known as 'proto-ionic', or 'proto-aeolic' (fig. XIV), of which examples had already been found at Meggido. These gave to the buildings the stamp of austere and stately magnificence.[2]

But there must certainly have been other fortified lines. Some alignments were actually found to the

[1] See Père Vincent, *RB*, 1946, p. 591.
[2] J. W. Crowfoot, *The Buildings at Samaria*, pp. 13–15.

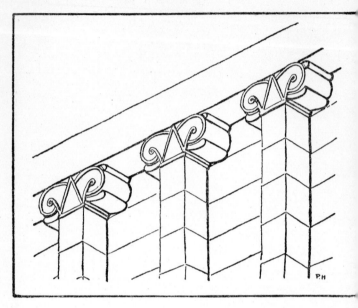

XIV. Proto-Ionic Pilasters (ibid. p. 15)

north of the casemated wall, and others to the south
of the 'basilica'.[1] This explains the protracted sieges
which the city was able to sustain, since it possessed
enclosed cultivable areas, and was therefore capable

---

[1] It would seem that this is the 'outer rampart' mentioned by
Père Vincent (*RB*, 1925, p. 438), enclosing an oval of about twenty
acres, whose measurements along the main axes were about 500
yards from east to west, and 300 yards from north to south. The
Roman city covered an area of about 160 acres. See below p. 107.

of prolonged resistance,[1] not, however, entirely escaping the horrors of famine.[2]

Only one gate belonging to the Israelite period has been located, at the eastern end:[3] a ramp with two right-angled turns gave access to the interior of the city. As was customary in the East, this gate was the scene of numerous episodes. There Ahab and Jehoshaphat consulted the prophets before attacking Ramoth-Gilead;[4] the four lepers sat there during the siege of the city by the Aramaeans;[5] and, lastly, the riotous sale of food took place there.[6]

Within these enclosures the site of the palace or palaces would naturally be found (fig. XV). It is held that three stages are discernible in the royal residence, ascribed respectively to Omri, Ahab, and Jeroboam II. What remains of Omri's palace had

[1] The siege under Ahab (I Kings 20), under Joram (II Kings 6.24 ff.), under Hoshea (II Kings 17.5-6), this last siege continued three years.

[2] II Kings 6.25-9, with the price of certain commodities, 80 shekels of silver for an ass's head; five shekels of silver for a minute portion of the herb star-of-Bethlehem (according to an ingenious theory of Père de Vaux, *Les Livres des Rois*, p. 145, note d.). But still more dreadful is the story that children were occasionally eaten. This shocking practice is alluded to elsewhere in the Bible, Deut. 28. 53-7; Lam. 4.10, but also in Accadian and Assyrian tablets, cf. *Iraq*, XVII (1955), p. 79. n. 34.

[3] Crowfoot, *op. cit.*, pp. 18-19, fig. 8.

[4] I Kings 22.10-12. It may be suggested that the 'horns of iron' which Zedekiah assumed, might have been an imitation of the horns on the headdress of the Canaanite Baals. For the place before the gate, cf. J. Gray, *The Krt Text*, p. 39.

[5] II Kings 7.3.

[6] II Kings 7.18-20.

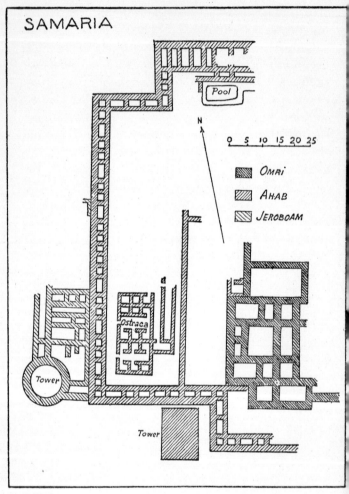

SAMARIA

Pool

N

0 5 10 15 20 25

Omri

Ahab

Jeroboam

Ostraca

Tower

Tower

XV. *The Israelite Palaces*
(*The round tower belongs to the Hellenistic period*)

been built over the group of neighbouring architectural court-rooms. Ahab developed this block of
buildings by enclosing it within the casemated wall.
Between the latter and a retaining wall built parallel
to it on the east, a rectangular building (31 m. 80 by
11 m. 30), with small square rooms and oblong
corridors, may have served for a storehouse. It was
here that the American expedition found a valuable
collection of ostraca.[1] Similarly, it was within the
palace enclosure that most of the ivories were discovered. These, if they had been intact, would have
been one of the finest collections ever yielded by an
excavation. What does remain of them is still of the
greatest importance.[2]

To the north of the court, built against the casemated wall, a rectangular reservoir was uncovered
(fig. XV) (10 m. 23 by 5 m. 20). Here, in all prob-
ability, stood the blood-stained chariot of Ahab, after
its return to Samaria from the siege of Ramoth-
gilead where he received a mortal wound. This will
have been 'the pool'[3] where the chariot was washed.

Outside, in a re-entrant on the south-west of the
casemated wall, a rectangular tower (16 m. by
12 m. 50) was also uncovered. The Hebrew term
(*armôn*) should be rendered 'citadel'. It may be

---

[1] For these ostraca, see below, p. 74.

[2] See below, p. 63.

[3] I Kings 22.38. This is the theory of R. Dussaud, 'Samarie au
Temps d'Achab', *Syria*, VI (1925), p. 324).

conjectured that the murder of Pekahiah took place here.[1]

The traces of Jeroboam's building are harder to determine. It is possible that this king restored the dwelling of his predecessors, but he may also have enlarged it. Perhaps he is responsible for a share of the buildings uncovered beyond the casemated wall, which seem to have belonged to the same extensive architectural complex of buildings. At any rate, it is to the latter that the Bible refers when it speaks of 'the ivory palaces'[2] which adorned the hill of Samaria. Light has been thrown on this expression by archaeology, since excavation of the site has yielded a large quantity of ornamental plaques used to decorate the furniture (beds, chairs, thrones, etc.) of this royal residence.[3]

*　　　*　　　*

[1] II Kings 15.25. This also is a theory of R. Dussaud, *loc. cit.*, p. 323, indicating, moreover, the existence of a castle at Tirzah, I Kings 16.18.

[2] I Kings 22.39; Amos 3.15; Ps. 14.9. Opinions differ as to the interpretation of this expression. Reisner, *op. cit.*, p. 61, thinks that the use of polished white limestone for the building sufficiently explains the origin of the title; R. Dussaud, *Syria*, 1926, p. 318, regards it as an 'official designation'. A Lods, in the *Bible du Centenaire*, on I Kings 22.39, thinks that the name 'arose from the extensive use of this precious material for the decoration of rooms and furniture'. Similarly de Vaux, in *Les Livres des Rois*, p. 122, note b. On the other hand, Crowfoot, *Early Ivories from Samaria*, p. 1, thinks of a hall of the palace, decorated with ivory panels, let into the walls.

[3] We believe that the designation has arisen from the presence, in the palace, of furniture decorated in this way. For the scale of the plaques is much too small for mural decoration.

The Samaria Ivories.[1] The Harvard University expedition had found some ivory fragments, all lying on the floor of the court of Ahab's palace.[2] One of them was picked up along with a fragment of ala-

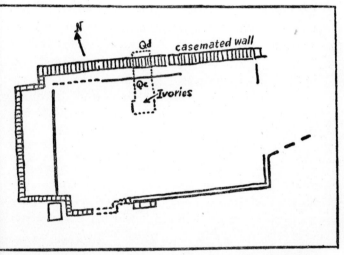

XVI. *Locality of the Ivories in the Palace (from Crowfoot,* Early Ivories from Samaria, *p. 3)*

---

[1] J. W. Crowfoot and Grace M. Crowfoot, *Early Ivories from Samaria*; C. Watzinger, *Denkmäler Palästinas*, I, pp. 112–14, Plate 37; A. G. Barrois, *Manuel d'archéologie biblique*, I, pp. 503–7; W. F. Albright, *The Archaeology of Palestine*, pp. 136–7, Plate 24; C. Decamps de Mertzenfeld, *Ivoires phéniciens*, pp. 62–75, Plates VIII-XXII; Vincent, in *RB*, 1939, pp. 633–7; R. D. Barnett, 'Phoenician and Syrian Ivory Carving', in *PEQ*, 1939, pp. 4 ff.; G. R. 'Ivory Carvings from Samaria received by Fogg Museum', *Art and Archaeology* (1934), p. 89.

[2] Reisner, *op. cit.*, p. 368, Plates 56 (c, f), 66 (h).

baster inscribed with the name of the Pharaoh
Osorkon II (870–847).[1] This gave a valuable syn-
chronism with the reign of Ahab (869–850).[2] This
treasure, however, was eclipsed by the harvest
gathered by Crowfoot's expedition. Nearly two hundred plaques, or fragments of plaques, were discovered in the course of his excavation from 1931 to
1935, and almost entirely within the royal enclosure.[3]
The most important group was closely bunched, and
in this area, according to the excavator, lay the 'ivory
house' referred to in the Bible. He was unable, however, to discover its ground-plan. This whole sector
showed traces of the destruction and the fire which
had ruined many of the plaques.

The plaques displayed various techniques: incised
designs, carving in low relief, fretwork, often en-
hanced by enamel inlay (lapis lazuli, glass), or by
gold-leaf overlay.[4] The result was a polychromatic

[1] E. Drioton and J. Vandier, *L'Egypte*, p. 631; Reisner, *op. cit.*,
Plate 56, g.

[2] Assuming, of course, that the level on which these documents
were discovered had not been disturbed in antiquity, a condition
frequently established by archaeologists in the course of excavation.

[3] The figures given by Crowfoot, *op. cit.*, p. 4, n. 3, are as follows:
out of 197 plaques or fragments, 184 come from Qc, 11 from Qk,
1 from Qn, 1 from Qf. There is a sketch of the site on p. 3 of Crowfoot's book.

[4] Thureau-Dangin, *Arslan-Tash*, p. 139, has pointed out that the
distinction between these two latter types of technique had been
indicated in the inscription of Adadnirari III, in his inventory of
the spoil of Damascus, where ivory inlay (*tamlû*) is distinguished from
ivory overlaid (*ihzu*). These techniques have received further illustration from the ivories found at Nimrud by Mallowan, cf. *Iraq*, XIV,
(1952), p. 47, Plate XIV.

effect, very pleasing to the eye[1] and avoiding the otherwise predominantly yellow tone of the decoration. To the lapis lazuli and enamel inlay must be added, according to Amos (3.15) the combination of ivory and ebony. This technique has been recently confirmed by the evidence of the Ras Shamra excavations.[2]

Here are some of the themes depicted on these plaques,[3] showing clear evidence of Egyptian influence:

1. *The infant Horus* (Plate 2) is seated on a lotus flower. In his right hand he holds the *flagellum* whose lashes lie over his right shoulder, and he is putting the fingers of his left hand in his mouth. The plaque was overlaid with blue and green enamel, touched up with gold.

2. *The infant Horus* in the same position, accompanied by the Egyptian god Ra (Plate 3), falcon-headed, kneeling, and offering with his left hand the figurine of Maat, the Egyptian goddess of Truth,

---

[1] There is certainly an allusion to this technique in S. of Sol. 5.14, 'His body is as bright ivory encrusted with sapphires.' This is referred to by Crowfoot, *op. cit.*, p. 10.

[2] The confirmation spoken of refers, not to the discovery of an object, but to an allusion in an inscription. On a cuneiform tablet of the thirteenth century B.C., which contains an inventory of the trousseau of Queen Ahatmilku, reference is made to 'a chair of ebony, inlaid with ivory'. Cf. J. Nougayrol, *Le palais d'Ugarit*, III, p. 184 (1955).

[3] Only the most typical examples are mentioned here.

but also possibly a symbol of material offerings.[1]

3. *The god Hah*, seated, with legs folded (Plate 4), holds in each hand a palm branch from which hangs an *ankh* sign. Above, a border of Phoenico-Cypriote palmettos frames the scene which continues on the right.

4. The Egyptian goddesses, *Isis and Nephthys* (Plate 5), are kneeling, facing one another on either side of a *ed* tree,[2] supported by a lotus flower, and crowned with a disc. The goddesses are protecting the symbolic emblem[3] with their wings.

5. *A Winged Sphinx*,[4] androcephalous (Plate 6), facing left, is moving towards a plant. A tongue is still attached to the upper and under side of these plaques, showing that they were once fitted into a larger whole.

---

[1] J. Vandier, *La religion égyptienne*, p. 166; A. Moret, 'Motifs dogmatiques égyptiennes à Samarie, Damas, Pasargade', in *Journal Asiatique*, 1936, pp. 485–7; 'Notice sur les plaques d'ivoire provenant du palais du roi Achab à Samarie', in *CRA*, 1936, pp. 19–20.

[2] An Egyptian symbol connected with the Osiris cult, where a tree-trunk with branches lopped often appears. For the *ded* tree see A. Moret, *Le Nil et la civilisation égyptienne*, p. 93; J. Vandier, *op. cit.*, pp. 189–90, 225.

[3] The theme of winged goddesses protecting an infant or a symbolic plant is of common occurrence. The finest examples are from Arslan Tash, Thureau-Dangin, *op. cit.*, Plates XIX-XXV. Christian hymnology still retains unsuspected traces of this imagery, as in the line, ' Beneath the shadow of thy wings thy saints have dwelt secure.'

[4] These are a prototype of the cherubim, frequently represented in the Temple at Jerusalem. Cf. *The Temple of Jerusalem*, p. 35 and fig. VIII.

6. *Criocephalous Sphinxes*,[1] winged, on each side of a palmetto.[2]

7. A *Lion* attacking a *Bull* (fig. XVIIa), and biting under its neck.[3]

8. *Lions*, carved in the round (fig. XVIIb), probably once decorating the arms of a throne.[4] On the back of the animals a rectangular insertion has been cut, intended to support the standing figure of an attribute or a deity. It is not surprising that numerous representations of this animal should have been found, since it was common in Palestine and particularly in the Samaritan countryside.[5]

9. *Stags in motion, and drinking*[6] (fig. XVIIc).

10. *Woman at the Window* (fig. XVIIIa). Only a single specimen of this type has been found, although

---

[1] i.e., ram-headed.

[2] A fine specimen of this type was found at Arslan Tash, Thureau-Dangin, *op. cit.*, Plate XXVII.

[3] A theme of frequent occurrence in oriental iconography, for which many explanations have been put forward: e.g., the lion, as a wild animal, in opposition to the bull, as a domestic animal; nomads as opposed to settled population; drought opposed to fertility; Ishtar opposed to Hadad, and so forth.

[4] Solomon's throne, of which there is a description in I Kings 10.19–20, was decorated with lions, two of which are mentioned as 'standing beside the stays' (I.C.C. 'arms').

[5] II Kings 17.25-6; Amos 3.4, 8.

[6] There is an obvious biblical parallel in Ps. 42.2, 'As a hart that panteth after the waterbrooks.' The rendering is open to modification. It may be rendered, 'as a hart that stretches out its neck towards the waterbrooks'. This corresponds exactly to the way in which the animal is represented on the plaque, stretching out towards the stream.

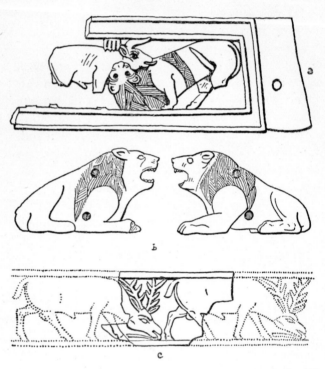

XVII. Samaria Ivories: (a) Lion attacking a Bull; (b) Lions carved in the round; (c) Stags drinking. (ibid., Pl. X, 1; IX, 1; X, 8a)

it is common on other sites.[1] It depicts a head emerg-
ing from an aperture framed with concentric bands.[2]

11. *A Figure seated on a Throne.* The piece is unfortunately very broken, but it can be seen from what
remains that the two men represented were bare-
foot. The seat had a high back and was uphol-
stered with a long cushion, doubled and folded over
the back of the chair. No doubt the scene would have
depicted a king and an attendant.

12. *Various Objects* (fig. XVIIIb, c, d). Many fragments depict vegetation or flowers: lotus, lilies, papyrus reeds, palmettos, marguerites, etc., which had
helped to compose borders, friezes, or metopes, in-
serted into various articles. It seems to us quite
certain that these served to decorate furniture, and
not as panelling of rooms.[3]

This sumptuous furniture speaks volumes for the
prosperity of the period. It was obviously the time of
Ahab, but doubtless of his successors also, among
others, Jehu, and especially Jeroboam II.[4] Indeed,

[1] Arslan Tash, Nimrud, Khorsabad. It is usually identified with
Venus παρακύπτουσα, soliciting the passers-by. It is possible to
connect the figure with 'the strange woman' of Prov. 2.16.

[2] This is no doubt a correct representation of the windows, often
mentioned in the Bible, and therefore resembling a wicket. Similarly,
we may imagine the head of Jezebel, framed by the window at
Jezreel, as she addressed Jehu (II Kings 9. 32). See above p. 37.

[3] This is also the opinion of Père Vincent, *RB*, 1939, p. 636, as
against J. W. and G. M. Crowfoot, *op. cit.*, p. 1.

[4] We differ, therefore, from those who think that all the ivories of
Samaria belong to the same period, namely, that of Ahab, as J. W.
and G. M. Crowfoot and Père Vincent, and we accept the view of

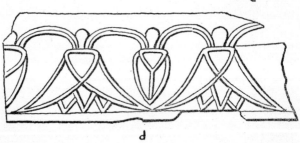

*XVIII. Samaria Ivories: (a) Woman at the Window;
(b) Stylized Palm-tree; (c) Palmettos; (d) Frieze of Lotus
(ibid., Pl. XIII, 2; p. 36; p. 40; Pl. XVI, 2)*

the reference to 'the ivory palace' built by Ahab,[1] and also to the 'beds of ivory'[2] on which, in the time of Jeroboam II, the nobles of Samaria took their ease,[3] are congruous with the dates assigned to these ornamental plaques, which are not all by the same hand, that is to say, from the same workshop, nor from the same period.[4]

The question also arises where these objects were made, for the site of their manufacture is in dispute. It may as well have been Samaria as the Phoenician coast, or even Damascus.[5]

Albright, *The Archaeology of Palestine*, p. 137, who distinguishes two groups, belonging respectively to the ninth and eighth centuries B.C. A.-G. Barrois, *Manuel d'archéologie biblique*, I, p. 506, does not seem positive; he speaks, however, of 'Ahab and his successors' (p. 503).

[1] I Kings 22.39.

[2] Amos 6.4. A couch, similarly decorated, was found at Ras Shamra in 1952, cf. Schaeffer, in *Syria*, XXXI (1954), p. 53 and Plates VII–X.

[3] It is not impossible that such persons possessed 'period' furniture, which might, therefore, have been older than the time of Jeroboam II (786–746).

[4] A sharp distinction must be made between the plaques (Crowfoot, *op. cit.*, Plate XI) with clearly defined faces, to which we assign a date in the first half of the ninth century, and others (*ibid.* Plates I–VI), related to the Arslan-Tash collection (second half of the ninth century), whose date is fixed by the mention of Hazael's name, who reigned about 842 B.C., and therefore after Ahab. Other ivories may have been executed in the eighth century (i.e., under Jeroboam II), in the opinion of such experts as R. D. Barnett, in *Iraq*, II (1935), p. 185, or M. E. Mallowan, *ibid.*, XIII (1951), p. 6. Some of the plaques bear inscriptions on the back in an archaic script (Hebrew, Phoenician, or Aramaic) which points to the ninth century B.C.

[5] The various wars between Samaria and Damascus were interrupted by intervals of peace when relations were resumed. This appears from some of the stories in the Elisha cycle (II Kings 5: the

However, the result was the same: not only were
many scandalized by this lavish display of wealth, in
view of the distress and poverty in which many members of the community were living,[1] but, above all,
the adherents of orthodox Jahvism saw that it was
inevitable for the ruling classes of Israel to become
corrupted by foreign religious beliefs, and by a
mythology and imagery which were definitely Egyptian.[2] Already the 'bulls of Jeroboam' were a sign of
compromise with Canaanite cults. In the sight of the
ruling classes and with royal approval, another pantheon was being exhibited, bringing to Samaria something far more sinister than a mere artistic display of
decorative imagination.

*   *   *

The Ostraca. Together with the ivories, the *ostraca*[3]
constitute a most valuable collection of documentary

healing of Naaman the Syrian; 8. 7–15: the journey of Elisha to
Damascus). Watzinger, *Denkmäler Palästinas*, I, p. 113, thinks of Tyre
and Damascus. The discovery of unfinished ivories implies, however,
that some of them were made in Samaria.

[1] Amos 2.6; 3.10; 4.1; 5.11.

[2] We have mentioned the various deities represented: Horus, Ra,
Hah, Isis, Nephthys. Osiris also appears on one fragment. The
Phoenician sea-board was more exposed to Egyptian influence than
inland Syria. However, the discovery under the mosque of the
Umayyads at Damascus of a large stone slab decorated with a sphinx
(*Syria*, XXVI (1949), pp. 191–5) shows clearly that the influence of
Egyptian iconography extended far inland, for this monument had
certainly been executed in Damascus. In addition, the type of sphinx
there depicted closely resembles the Samarian example.

[3] Mention may also be made of the pottery fragments of broken
utensils, bearing alphabetic signs in ink or engraved with a stylus.

material. Most of them were found by the Harvard Expedition in a building situated, as has been said,[1] between the palace of Omri and the casemated wall, on the west. They were edited by G. A. Reisner,[2] and have been the subject of many studies[3] which need not be discussed here. But their scope affords evidence of the historical, philological, cultural, and religious value of these insignificant fragments of clay which have been so fortunately preserved for us.

The collection discovered by the Americans consists of sixty-five pieces, of which sixty-three have inscriptions in ink, and two are incised. It is supposed that they are invoices accompanying taxes in kind despatched by the overseers to the royal storehouses.[4] These invoices are dated by various regnal years of a

[1] See above p. 59.

[2] *Israelite Ostraca from Samaria* (no date), and *Harvard Excavations at Samaria*, pp. 227–46, Plate 55.

[3] Père Abel, 'Un mot sur les ostraca de Samarie', in *RB*, 1911, pp. 290–3; *Géographie de la Palestine*, II, pp. 95–7; W. F. Albright, in *JPOS*, V, 1925, pp. 38–43; 1936, p. 248 f.; R. Dussaud, 'Samarie au temps d'Achab,' in *Syria*, VI (1925), pp. 314–38; VII (1926), pp. 9–29; H. Gressmann, in *ZATW* (1925), pp. 147–50; D. Diringer, *Le Iscrizioni antico-ebraiche Palestinesi* (1934), pp. 21–74; M. Noth, 'Der Beitrag der samarischen Ostraca zur Lösung topographischer Fragen', in *Palästina Jahrbuch*, 1932, pp. 54–67; B. Maisler, 'Der Distrikt Srq in den samarischen Ostraca?' in *JPOS*, XIV, (1934), pp. 96–100; 'The Historical Background of the Samaria Ostraca', in *JPOS*, XXII (1948), pp. 117–33; S. Moscati, *L'epigraphia ebraica antica* (1951), pp. 27–39; K. Galling, *Textbuch zur Geschichte Israels*, p. 50.

[4] Albright, in *JPOS*, V, p. 42, has shown that the formula prescribed for the drawing-up of these invoices was as follows: In the year X—from such and such a place—to overseer X—from taxpayer X.

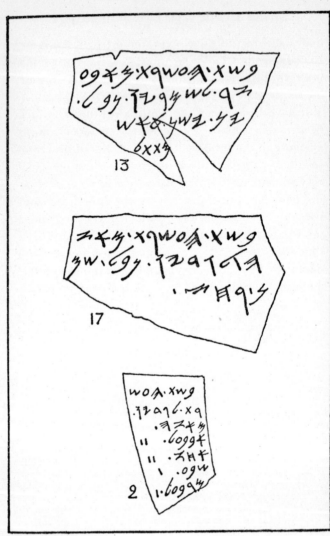

XIX. Ostraca 13, 17, 2 (from HES, p. 239)

king whose name has been omitted: the years are the ninth, tenth, fifteenth, and seventeenth.[1] We possess the names of a dozen of the overseers,[2] as well as that of the town from which they were despatched, and the persons who paid them. The dues were paid in wine and oil.

The inscription on ostracon 13 (fig. XIX) reads: 'In the tenth year (sent from the town) of Abi'ezer to Shemario, a jar of old wine. To Ish (a, a jar of old wine) from the town of Tetel.' On ostracon 17 we read: 'In the tenth year (sent from the town) of Azzah to Gaddio, a jar of fine oil'.[3]

Wine and oil are the two products coupled together by Amos in his oracle which brings the charge against the people of Samaria that, 'they drink wine in bowls, and anoint themselves with the finest oil.'[4]

A study of the onomasticon yields interesting information. It discloses the fact, already suspected, of the dissemination of foreign cults among the popula-

[1] R. Dussaud, *loc. cit.*, p. 27, emends 17 to 13, and 15 to 11.

[2] From this is might be inferred that the kingdom of Israel was organized for purposes of taxation on lines similar to those in Solomon's times: namely, an overseer who was responsible for the maintenance of the royal household during one month (I Kings 4.7). On this point see R. Dussaud, *loc. cit.*, p. 28.

[3] The term *shemen raḥaṣ* is new. Reisner translates it 'fine oil'. R. Dussaud adopts this rendering, and points out that the oil in question is intended for anointing the body (*loc. cit.*, p. 25). Diringer is of the same opinion, *op. cit.*, p. 38, as Père Savignac points out in *RB*, 1935, p. 292. The latter gives another rendering: 'refined oil'.

[4] Amos 6.6.

tion. Such names appear as: Abiba'al, Meriba'al,[1] Ba'almeoni, Ba'alazakar, but the persistence of theophorous names compounded with Jahveh, such as Joiada', Joiashib, Jo'ash, Gaddijô, 'Egeljô,[2] shows, however, that Jahvism remained firmly entrenched among a population which followed the example of its rulers.[3]

Together with names of persons there occur place-

*XX. 'Seal of Shema', servant of Jeroboam
(from H. Gressmann, AOB II, 578)*

names[4] of which the most familiar is Shechem, to the south of Samaria, and the majority of them are near

---

[1] The name of one of Jonathan's sons (I Chron. 8.34), changed by the compilers into Mephibosheth (II Sam. 4.4). Both these names are on ostracon 2 (fig. XIX).

[2] '*Egeljô* might be rendered 'Jahveh is a young bull', suggesting the cult at Bethel. This remark is from Père Abel, *loc. cit.*, p. 293.

[3] This is also borne out by the names of several of Ahab's sons (see above, pp. 32–3).

[4] Several identifications have been suggested by Abel, Dussaud, and Albright, but only a few by Reisner.

the capital. However, the occurrence of the name No'ah, assuming that the site has been correctly identified,[1] suggests that the most northerly districts were not exempt from these requisitions upon which the provisioning of the capital depended.

In the first flush of the discovery, and relying on the presence in this sector of the jar-fragment bearing the name of the Pharaoh Osorkon II (870–847), the conclusion was reached that the ostraca belonged to the reign of Ahab.[2] But comparative epigraphy has raised various chronological difficulties which have not yet been surmounted. The resumption of excavation by Crowfoot's expedition brought about changes in the architectural dating which necessitated the lowering of the date of the ostraca, so that it is now generally agreed that they should be assigned to the period of Jeroboam II (786–746 B.C.)[3] To the time of the same king we should, with equal certainty, assign the fine seal discovered some time ago at Megiddo

[1] R. Dussaud identifies it with Nain (Luke 7.11), hence beyond the plain of Jezreel. So, too, Diringer. The identification is questioned by Père Savignac, *RB* 1935, p. 292.

[2] The excavators had, however, allowed a wider chronological margin when they spoke of Ahab's palace as being occupied from about 865 to 722 B.C. (*HES*, p. 227). For this Egyptian gift to Samaria see Alan Rowe, in the *Journal of the Manchester University Egyptian and Oriental Society*, XXV, 1947–53 (1954).

[3] Diringer still prefers a high date (867–859 B.C.), although B. Maisler has proposed the reign of Jehoahaz. Albright, in *The Archaeology of Palestine*, p. 129, assigns them to the period of Jeroboam II; M. Noth in *Die Welt des Alten Testaments*, p. 174, places them in the first half of the eighth century; K. Galling, *Textbuch*, p. 30, assigns them to the reign of Joash (802–787).

and engraved with the name 'Shema, servant of Jeroboam'.[1] Its lion, with yawning mouth, admirably illustrates the well-known utterance of the prophet: 'The lion hath roared, who will not fear.'[2]

The rest of the epigraphic material which can be assigned to the royal period[3] is very limited: there is a fragment of an Israelite stele, a mere splinter, on which are three letters (*a*, *š*, *r*)[4]; the remains of an Assyrian stele, made of the local stone, with a much defaced inscription; possibly, also, a few tiles, bearing Aramaic letters, which were found by one or other of the expeditions.[5]

*　　　*　　　*

We have seen how the architecture, the ivories, the ostraca, enable us to reconstruct the daily life of the court of Samaria; but there is a class of objects, insignificant, yet even more important, which claims our attention, and that is the pottery. In reading some of the Bible narratives, it would be interesting to know the shape of some of the receptacles mentioned. One example may suffice: in the account[6] of

---

[1] Schumacher, *Tell el-Mutesellim*, I, p. 99, fig. 147. This seal has often been reproduced (cf. H. Gressmann, *Altorientalische Bilder zum Alten Testament*, 578), as it well deserves to be.

[2] Amos 3.8.

[3] An account will be given later, p. 93, of certain documents which belong to the period between the capture of the city by the Assyrians (722 B.C.) and the arrival of Alexander (332 B.C.).

[4] Sukenik, 'Note on a Fragment of an Israelite Stele found at Samaria', in *PEQ*, 1936, p. 156.

[5] For these tiles see below p. 92.   [6] I Kings 17.

Elijah's sojourn at Zarephath with the widow, three different pieces of pottery are mentioned. There is the crock (*keli*) for water;[1] the jar (*kad*) for flour,[2] and the jug (*sappahath*) for oil.[3] No doubt these vessels differed from one another in capacity and shape. But it is very difficult, among the archaeological material at our disposal, to single out and name cor-

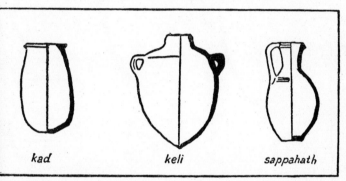

kad   *keli*   *sappahath*

XXI. Israelite Jars and Ewer: kad, keli, sappahath

rectly these vessels which the biblical narratives have carefully distinguished.[4]

We have suggested here three types (fig. **XXI**) which may correspond to the receptacles which the Bible designates respectively, *keli*, *kad*, and *sappahath*.

[1] I Kings 17.10.   [2] I Kings 17.12.   [3] I Kings 17.12.
[4] J. L. Kelso and J. Palin Thorley, *Palestinian Pottery in Bible Times;* James Kelso, 'The Ceramic Vocabulary of the Old Testament' (*BASOR, Supplementary Studies*, No. 5–6); K. Galling, *Biblisches Reallexikon*, art. *Keramik*, col. 314–30; Barrois, *Manuel d'archéologie biblique*, I, pp. 442–5.

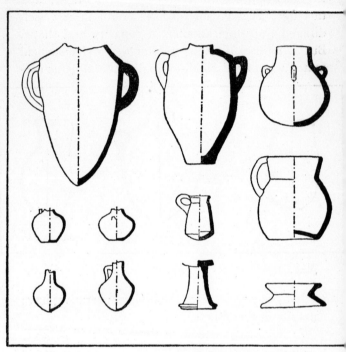

XXII. Israelite Pottery found at Samaria (from HES, p. 276)

8. *Street with Colonnades*

9. *Staircase of the Temple of Augustus*

Moreover, the nobles of Samaria, according to Amos, drank wine out of 'bowls'.[1] These must surely have been more elegant receptacles than the specimens of ordinary pottery (fig. XXII) picked up on every site in a more or less complete state of preservation.

*　　　*　　　*

It is useless to attempt to distinguish what is Israelite among the vast quantity of metal objects, tools or ornaments, because of the impossibility of dating the stratigraphy with any certainty. It would be interesting to be able to identify examples of Israelite military equipment in the time of Ahab, Jehu, or Jeroboam II, and to study the jewels which might have adorned the foreheads, the ears, the necks, or the hands of the nobles of Samaria, or of those 'cows of Bashan'[2] against whom Amos fulminated. All that we can identify with certainty is the representation of those 'hooks' and 'fish hooks' with which Amos threatened them.[3] These we find depicted on many Assyrian reliefs which represent the victorious king holding a cord attached to a ring passed through the upper lip of his conquered foes.[4] Sargon, the conqueror of Samaria, is represented in this attitude,[5] the brutality of which is intensified by the fact

---

[1] Amos 6.6. The term is '*miz^eraq*'.　　　[2] Amos 6.1.

[3] Amos 4.2.

[4] For illustrations of this point it is usual to refer to the steles of Esarhaddon discovered at Zenjirli and Tell Ahmar (see *Nineveh and the Old Testament*, p. 64–5, and fig. XIV).

[5] The palace of Khorsabad, room 8, relief No. 12 (fig. XXIII).

F　　　　　　　　　　[81]

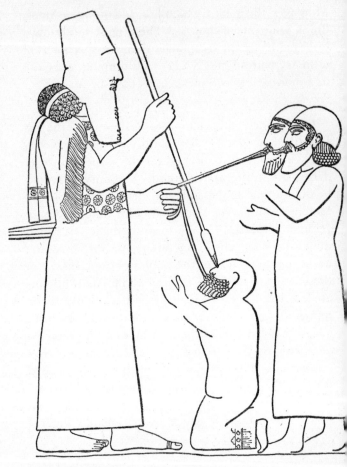

XXIII. Sargon II puts out the eyes of an enemy held on a leash (Botta, Monument de Ninive, *Pl. 118)*

that the king is thrusting out the eyes of his kneeling adversary.[1]

We do not know the ultimate fate of Hoshea, the last king of Samaria. He may have been imprisoned, deported like his subjects, or executed like many of them. In any case, whether his death was slow or violent, it made no difference to the fortunes of the State. Israel might have ceased to exist as a nation, but the history of Samaria continued.

---

[1] This will have been the punishment inflicted on Zedekiah, king of Judah, in the sixth century, when he was taken to Riblah, where Nebuchadrezzar had his headquarters (II Kings 25.6–7; Jer. 52.10–11). There is also a direct reference to this mode of treatment in Isa. 37.29; Ezek. 29.4; 38.4.

III

SAMARIA IN THE
ASSYRIAN, BABYLONIAN, AND
HELLENISTIC PERIODS

WHEN Samaria fell after a siege of three years, the
Assyrians followed their usual practice of deporting
the major part of the population,[1] and carried off the
plunder of the conquered city to their palaces on the
banks of the Tigris.[2]

This policy of depopulation was then succeeded by
a process of repopulation. Sargon brought into
Samaria a body of settlers from previously conquered
territories. On this point biblical tradition and
Assyrian records are in complete agreement. The
two accounts of this event are given below in parallel
columns:

[1] We have already seen the number of the prisoners according to
the Assyrian records (see above, p. 51).

[2] The possibility must be admitted that the ivories found in the
palace of Khorsabad, the residence of Sargon, may actually have
come from Samaria and from 'the ivory house' of the biblical records.
For these ivories see G. Loud, *Khorsabad*, II, pp. 96–7 and Plates
51–4. The ivories are of the following types: woman at the window
(nine examples), winged sphinx passant (fifteen examples), winged
goddesses (three examples). However, not a single Aramaic or
Phoenician letter has been noticed in the collection.

THE PRISM OF SARGON[1]	II KINGS 17.24
I rebuilt the city of Samaria, and made it greater than it was before. I settled there a population from the countries which I myself had conquered. I appointed my officer as governor over them, and I reckoned them among the people of Assyria.	And the king of Assyria brought men from Babylon,[2] and from Cuthah,[3] and from Avva,[4] and from Hamath,[5] and Sepharvaim,[6] and placed them in the cities of Samaria instead of the children of Israel; and they possessed Samaria, and dwelt in the cities thereof.

In spite of all these precautions, the beginnings of the occupation were marked by disturbances. The country had not been entirely depopulated, and it attempted to throw off the Assyrian yoke. The name of Samaria is to be found among the revolted peoples who had assembled their forces at the instigation of Ilubi'di. Those enumerated are Arpad, Simirra,

[1] The text was found at Nimrud and published in *Iraq*, XVI, (1954), p. 180. It confirms other well-known and often quoted texts (cf. Pritchard, *ANET*, p. 284).

[2] At Babylon Sargon had crushed the rebellion of Marduk-apaliddin (=Merodach-baladan, Isa. 39.1.).

[3] The modern Tell Ibrahim, about 20 miles north-west of Babylon. It was the seat of the worship of Nergal.

[4] The site has not been identified. Perhaps in Elam, cf. Dhorme in *RB*, 1910, p. 376.

[5] The modern Hama on the Orontes, in central Syria. Sargon has given us the name of the king of this city: Jaubi'di (or Ilubi'di).

[6] Perhaps Sibraim (Ezek. 47.16) between Hamath and Damascus. This passage of II Kings 17.24, should be compared with Isa. 37. 12–13.

Damascus, Gaza and Samaria,[1] aided by Egypt. The movement failed and was brutally repressed. The chief instigator, Hanno of Gaza, was marked out for special treatment, and was sent in chains to Ashur.

The change of government was accompanied by further misfortunes. The new settlers were troubled by lions[2] sent by Jahveh to devour them. A report was sent to the Assyrian king, who immediately gave orders that one of the deported priests should be sent back to his own country to instruct the new population in the worship due to the god of Israel.[3] This representative of the priesthood, on returning to Israel, settled at Bethel[4], where he taught the inhabitants how Jahveh should be worshipped.

The new settlers, however, were not satisfied with the cult of Jahveh, but remained faithful to their own deities. Henceforward Samaria becomes the scene of

[1] *ANET*, p. 285. The account of this insurrection is given in two different sources, the Annals, and the Chronicles. Dhorme has commented on these texts in *RB*, 1910, pp. 377–8.

[2] Some commentators have regarded this increase in the wild animals as the result of the decrease in the cultivation of the depopulated areas due to wars, cf. *The Westminster Dictionary of the Bible*, p. 528.

[3] According to contemporary ideas people were supposed to worship the god of the country in which they were living. This is explicitly stated in I Sam. 26.19.

[4] The choice of Bethel rather than Samaria is significant. In the kingdom of Israel Bethel was the centre of the national religion. Cf. Amos 7.13. No doubt, as W. F. Albright points out in *Archaeology and the Religion of Israel*, p. 172, the Assyrian governor wished to counteract the still existing attraction which the Temple at Jerusalem exercised upon the inhabitants of the land.

the proliferation of foreign cults, where widely differing religions meet and mingle. Jeroboam I, it may be remembered, had filled his kingdom with shrines.[1] The settlers took them over and set up their idols in them. The biblical accounts give their names,[2] sometimes in altered forms, rendering identification difficult. Thus the Babylonians had set up Succoth-benoth,[3] the people from Cuthah, Nergal,[4] those from Hamath, Ashima;[5] those from Avva installed Nibhaz and Tartak.[6] The deities of Sepharvaim were known under the names of Adrammelech and Anam-melech.[7]

---

[1] I Kings 12.31.

[2] II Kings 17.30–31.

[3] According to Dhorme, *loc. cit.*, p. 375, the name is to be explained as *Sakkut* (the name of a planet sacred to Marduk) and *Zerbanit* (=Sarpanit, the consort of Marduk).

[4] The god of fire and of the underworld, represented as a warrior, with a mace in one hand, and a harpé in the other. A fine example was found in our excavation of Larsa, *Glyptique mésopotamienne*, 260.

[5] According to Dhorme, *loc. cit.*, p. 376, a small emendation (*r* instead of *m*), would give us the name *Asherah*, a goddess worshipped by all the western Semites. On the other hand, A. Lods identifies this goddess of Hamath with *Ashemah* of Samaria, mentioned in Amos 8.14 (R.V. 'the *sin* of Samaria'), or with *Ashim-Bethel*, worshipped by the Jews of Elephantiné, cf. A. Vincent, *La religion des Judéo-Araméens d'Eléphantine*, p. 545, 654. For the latter it is the name of a god, not of a goddess.

[6] Most of the commentators offer no identification. Dhorme, *loc. cit.*, proposes the Elamite god *Huban* (var. *Humban*). For Tartak, Montgomery, *The Books of Kings* (1951), suggests Atargatis, as Eiss-feldt reminds us in *VT*, III (1955), p. 102, n. 1.

[7] These are doubtless the Syrian deities Hadad and Anat. On this point, cf. O. Eissfeldt, 'Adrammelek und Demarus', in *La Nouvelle Clio*, VII (1955), pp. 153–9.

The first wave of colonists settled by Sargon in Samaria was succeeded by others, in the time of Esarhaddon (680–669),[1] and even in the time of Ashurbanipal (668–631).[2] Further intermixture of races took place, causing increased religious syncretism.[3] The inevitable result was obvious. Early Jahvism, which had previously been exposed to the rivalry of the Canaanite pantheon, was now in danger of being submerged under a tide of Mesopotamian cults. The outcome seemed unavoidable, and was only prevented by important political events. The Assyrian kingdom, struggling with serious internal disorders,[4] was no longer able to exercise its previous control over those peripheral provinces, known to the central administration at Nineveh as Samerina (Samaria) and Magidu (Megiddo). This is why it was possible for the king of Judah, Josiah (640–609), to advance into the former kingdom of Israel, and to destroy the temples and high places,[5] in the interests of the religious reforms which he had instituted at Jerusalem (621 B.C.). This purge encouraged

[1] Ezra 4.2.

[2] Ezra 4.9–10. 'Asnapper' is probably Ashurbanipal. The settlers whom he placed in Samaria, came from Babylonia, Erech (a Sumerian city), Elam, and Susa.

[3] This should not be forgotten if the 'Samaritan' religion is to be understood.

[4] We have given details in *Nineveh and the Old Testament*, pp. 76–87.

[5] II Kings 23.15–20; II Chron. 34.6–7. Since these shrines which went back to the Israelite period, had been re-occupied by foreign settlers, we may be certain that the various foreign cults which had been established there would not have escaped Josiah's attentions.

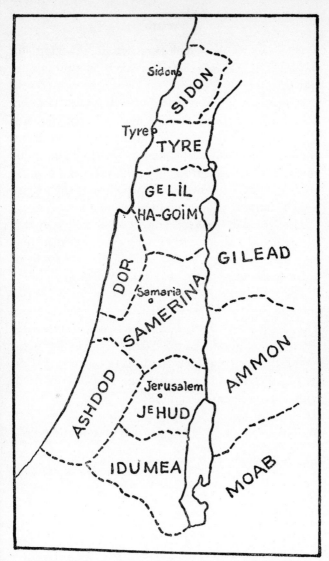

XXIV. *Palestine in the Achaemenid Period (from Abel,*
Géographie de la Palestine, *II, map VII)*

those Israelites who had been left in the land, to continue in, or to return to, an uncompromising Jahvism.

Hence it is not surprising to hear that, after the destruction of Jerusalem by the Neo-Babylonians (586 B.C.), a company of northern pilgrims from Shiloh, Shechem, and Samaria, should have journeyed in sackcloth, bringing to the ruins of Jahveh's house the offerings and incense which were the tokens of their faithful adherence to his worship.[1]

The Neo-Babylonian regime was succeeded by the Achaemenid rule, together with a new redistribution of territory (fig. XXIV), and permission granted to the exiles to return to Palestine (538 B.C.).

The difficulties they encountered on their return, and the opposition they met with, are well known. The latter was disastrous, and increased in intensity when the rebuilding of the Temple began. The representatives of the settlers, that is to say, the descendants of the Assyrian colonists who had intermarried with the indigenous inhabitants, proposed to the 'children of the Exile'[2] that they should be allowed to share in the work. The offer was unhesitatingly re-

In opposition to Albright, *The Biblical Period*, p. 45, we doubt whether the activities of the king of Judah in the Assyrian provinces of Samaria and Megiddo (territories of the former State of Israel), were carried on as a vassal of the kings of Nineveh. He merely took advantage of their weakened condition.

[1] Jer. 41.4–5.
[2] This was the designation of the returned exiles (cf. Ezra 4.1).

jected by the Jewish leaders, Zerubbabel and Joshua,[1] who declared their intention of carrying out the work unaided. Conciliation having been rejected, the breach was inevitable. Once more a state of schism was declared, and the Jewish State finally rejected the opportunity of restoring its religious unity.

However, the Samaritans had not abandoned their attempt. They used all the means in their power to render the task of the Jews more difficult. At first they succeeded through the help of the Persian governor, Rehum.[2] By the orders of the Achaemenid monarch the work was stopped, but King Darius (522–485 B.C.) rescinded the interdict.[3] In five years the House of Jahveh was rebuilt (520–515).

Fresh difficulties arose when the rebuilding of the walls began. This time the leader of the opposition was Sanballat, the Horonite,[4] who did not shrink from using warlike means to hinder the work.[5] Thanks to the energy of Nehemiah, who had the

---

[1] Ezra 4.3. The name Zerubbabel is clearly Babylonian: *Zer-Babel*=offspring of Babel.   [2] Ezra 4.8.

[3] See *The Temple of Jerusalem*, p. 70.

[4] Neh. 2.10. This man from Beth-Horon was the governor of Samaria. We learn this from the Elephantiné Papyri. See below p. 93 f. The enmity between Nehemiah and Sanballat probably had its origin in a question of precedence: the district of Judah which at first had been placed under the governor of Samaria, had been detached and placed under a separate authority. This has been clearly recognized by A. Alt, *Kleine Schriften*, II, p. 332, followed by M. Noth, *Histoire d'Israël*, p. 362. It is significant that Nehemiah refrained from addressing Sanballat by his official title, which clearly suggests an attitude of contempt.   [5] Neh. 4.7–8.

backing of the Persian king, this threat was averted, and Jerusalem with its Temple was now protected by fortified walls. The attempt at intimidation had completely failed. It should, however, be pointed out that certain influential people, who were almost certainly adherents of Jahvism,[1] were definitely thrown into opposition. Their Jahvism was discounted, and the rigorist Jewish party carried the day.

The excavation of Samaria has yielded scanty material illustrative of this period. Mention should, however, be made of a cuneiform tablet, in Neo-Babylonian, addressed to the local governor, Abi-Akhi;[2] also of the Assyrian pottery,[3] and of a series of inscribed tiles, some coming from the earlier excava-

[1] Sanballat bore a theophorous name whose meaning is obvious: *Sinuballit* 'the god Sin gives life'. But he had given purely Jewish names to his sons: Delaiah (= 'Jahveh has saved') and Shelemiah (= 'Jahveh is peace' or 'Jahveh has replaced', cf. A. Vincent, *La religion des Judéo-Araméens d'Eléphantine*, p. 415). The son-in-law of the same Sanballat was a grandson of Eliashib, the high priest of Jerusalem (Neh. 13.28). The ally of Sanballat, Tobiah (= 'Jahveh is my good') the Ammonite, had called his son Jehohanan (= 'Jahveh is gracious'). It is impossible to ignore the significance of these names.

[2] *HES*, p. 247 and Plate 56b. An order to Abi-akhi to provide the governor-general with five oxen and twelve sheep. We know the names of two Assyrian governors: Nabu-mukin-akhi, eponym in 690, and Nabu-shar-akhkhêshu, eponym after 648. The two names are in Albright, *Archaeology and the Religion of Israel*, p. 222, n. 139. Detailed references in *AfO*, XVII (1954-5), pp. 104, 118. See also A. Alt, in *Palästinajahrbuch*, 37 (1941), pp. 102–4 (quoted by M. Noth, *Histoire d'Israël*, p. 271, n. 4) and *Kleine Schriften*, II, p. 320.

[3] The American archaeologists have not observed the distinction in their comprehensive designation 'Babylonio-Grecian Pottery, 700–300 B.C.' Cf. *BASOR*, 135 (1954), p. 18 for comparisons with the 'Assyrian' pottery found at Dothan and Far'ah.

tions,[1] and some collected by Crowfoot's expedition.[2] All these fragments are hard to decipher, and Sukenik's interpretations (he believed that he had found the name of Jahveh on them),[3] were vigorously criticized at first,[4] but have subsequently met with some acceptance. The fragments have also given us some Bible names[5] which have supplemented the list of names already mentioned.

Although the soil of Samaria has yielded little material illustrative of this period, it should be pointed out that epigraphic documents discovered, often at a considerable distance from Israel, have furnished information concerning some of the persons mentioned in the biblical narrative.

We have already mentioned the names of Delaiah and Shelemiah, the sons of the governor, Sanballat, to whom, in the seventeenth year of Darius II (423–404 B.C.), the Jews settled at Elephantiné in Upper

---

[1] *HES*, pp. 247–8 and Plate 58.

[2] E. L. Sukenik, 'Inscribed Hebrew and Aramaic Potsherds from Samaria', in *PEQ*, 1933, pp. 152–6; 'Inscribed Potsherds with Biblical Names from Samaria', *ibid.* ,pp. 200–204; 'Potsherds from Samaria inscribed with the Divine Name,' *ibid.*, 1936, pp. 34–7.

[3] The same expert had, however, somewhat altered his readings, giving *Jehud* (Judaea), instead of *Iô* or *Iehô*, an abbreviated form of Jahveh.

[4] Père Vincent, who had at first sharply questioned the reading Jahveh (*RB*, 1937, pp. 632–3), seems afterwards to have defended it (*RB*, 1949, pp. 288–91) when Sukenik had abandoned it.

[5] Among them are: 'Uzza, 'Ezer, Ahaziah, Jojesha', Baruch (ostracon c 1101, for which Albright has suggested a complete reading, in *PEQ*, 1936, pp. 211–15).

Egypt had addressed a petition. They asked him to intervene on their behalf to obtain permission for them to rebuild the temple of Jahveh which had been destroyed by the local inhabitants.[1]

As we have already seen, another name among those allied with Sanballat and opposed to the returned exiles was that of Tobiah the Ammonite.[2] The same name has been found in a papyrus from the Fayum, belonging to the records of a certain Zeno, contemporary with Ptolemy II Philadelphus (285–246).[3] This Tobiah, who is styled 'governor of Ammon', can hardly be identified with Sanballat's colleague, but may very possibly be his descendant. At Araq el-Emir there is a hypogeum belonging to the Tobiad family, if we may credit the inscription on the rock.[4]

The name of Geshem the Arabian, which had been found in a Lihyan inscription, where he was associated with the Persian governor of Dedan, has recently turned up on a silver vessel acquired by the Brooklyn Museum, and which had been formerly dedicated to the Arabian goddess Han-'ilath by a certain 'Cain, the son of Geshem, the king of Kedar.' It is very pos-

[1] A. Cowley, *Aramaic Papyri of the Fifth Century B.C.*, p. 113; A. Vincent, *La Religion des Judéo-Araméens d'Eléphantine*, pp. 383–4; *ANET*, p. 492.

[2] Neh. 2.19.

[3] Millar Burrows, *What Mean These Stones?*, p. 111.

[4] The date of the hypogeum is disputed: Père Vincent places it in the third century B.C.; W. F. Albright at the end of the fifth century. Cf. Unger, *Archaeology and the Old Testament*, p. 311.

sible that this Geshem is the one mentioned in the book of Nehemiah.[1]

* * *

The breach between Samaria and Judaea was now final, and was given external sanction by the erection on Mount Gerizim of a temple 'like the Temple of Jerusalem'.[2] According to the Jewish historian Josephus, this event took place about 325 B.C.,[3] that is to say, after the conquest of Palestine by Alexander, and hence after the downfall of the Persian regime. The prime mover in this step was the governor Sanballat, who would appear to have made his son-in-law Manasseh the first priest[4] of the Samaritan cult, with the approval of the Greek monarch.[5] If it was Sanballat who carried out this act, it is doubtful whether he could have done it in the time of Alexander, for it is unlikely that a man would have been living and active in 325 B.C., who, as we know from the Elephantiné papyri[6] and the book of

[1] Frank M. Cross, Jr., in *BA*, XVIII (1955), p. 47.

[2] *Jewish Antiquities*, XIII, 9, 1.

[3] According to Josephus, the temple of Gerizim, destroyed about 125 B.C. by John Hyrcanus, lasted for two hundred years. If it was ever rebuilt the date is unknown.

[4] According to Neh. 13.28, the son of Joiada and grandson of Eliashib, the high priest of Jerusalem, was the son-in-law of Sanballat. He was expelled for having made a mixed marriage.

[5] *Jewish Antiquities*, XI, 7, 2; 8, 2, 4.

[6] A relevant contemporary example is the grand vizier of Morocco, el-Mokri, whose age oscillates between 102 and 109 years.

Nehemiah, was already active more than a century previously![1]

Nevertheless, there can be no doubt that the expulsions from Jerusalem carried out under the intolerant rule of Nehemiah and Ezra, brought about the collection at Samaria, not only of people of the lower classes, but also of important people, some of priestly rank, a situation which was favourable to the installation of a schismatic cult in the midst of a mixed population.[2] This cult was based upon a sacred book, the Torah, that is, the Pentateuch, brought from Jerusalem by one of the refugee Jewish priests,[3] and which furnished the necessary scriptural foundation for the new cult. It is noteworthy, in view of the enmity which henceforth separated Jews and

[1] The seventeenth year of Darius II (424–405 B.C.) would be about 407 B.C., hence the Jews of Elephantiné were petitioning his children. A way out of this difficulty is to suppose that there were two governors of Samaria with the name Sanballat. Rowley, in a paper read before the *Journées bibliques de Louvain* (Sept. 1954), attempts, however, to reconcile the statements of Josephus with those of the other sources (Nehemiah, Elephantiné). Cf. 'Sanballat and the Samaritan Temple', in *BJRL*, Sept. 1955. Josephus would appear to have post-dated the events which took place during the period of Nehemiah. On the same subject see a recent study by M. H. Segal, 'The Marriage of a High-Priest's Son to the Daughter of Sanballat and the Building of the Temple of Gerizim', in *Sefer Assaf*, 1953.

[2] It is very difficult to fix the date of the building of the temple of Gerizim. It can neither be placed as late as the Maccabaean period (Hölscher), or the first century B.C. (Albright), nor as early as the Persian period. We should be willing to place it in the beginning of the fourth century, perhaps under Artaxerxes II Mnemon (405–358). For the whole discussion see Rowley, in *BJRL*, Sept. 1955.

[3] G. Ricciotti, *Histoire d'Israël*, II, p. 193.

10. *The Basilica*

11. *Mount Gerizim*

12. *Mount Ebal*

Samaritans, that the former were never able to accuse the latter of idolatry,[1] as they certainly would have done if the worship of 'the calves' had been set up at Gerizim, or that of the images of the gods set up by the first settlers, after the fashion of Syria or Babylonia.[2] Hence their ritual and their religion bore the stamp of the strictness and exclusiveness of Jahvism. When Jesus met the Samaritan woman at Jacob's well, she could exclaim without shame or fear of blame: 'Our fathers worshipped in this mountain;[3] and ye say that in Jerusalem is the place where men ought to worship.'[4] In his reply Jesus did not claim the pre-eminence for Jerusalem, which would not have been surprising, but uttered the unexpected words: 'Neither in this mountain, nor yet in Jerusalem!'[5]

From the advent of Alexander (332 B.C.) to the Roman period (63 B.C.) our knowledge of the history of Samaria is scanty. The Greek conqueror was obliged to suppress a revolt shortly after he had passed through, and to avenge the murder of Andro-

[1] G. Ricciotti, *op. cit.*, II, p. 194.

[2] *Supra*, p. 16.

[3] Gerizim. For the cultic history of this mountain and the successive temples which were built on it (Samaritan, Roman, Christian), reference may be made to the article 'Garizim' by P. Antoine, in the *Dictionnaire de la Bible, Supplément*, col. 550–61. Today, the Samaritan community at Nablus, which has survived for several millennia (there were 160 Samaritans in 1939), celebrates Passover each year on Gerizim. For an account of this ceremony see J. Creten, 'La Pâque des Samaritains', in *RB*, 1922, pp. 434–42.

[4] John 4.20.   [5] John 4.21.

machus who had been killed by the Samaritans.[1] The
city was punished; a number of its inhabitants were
deported and replaced by Syro-Macedonian colonists.

After the death of Alexander, Palestine became
the theatre of the predatory activities of the Dia-
dochi.[2] Ptolemy I, king of Egypt, took Jerusalem and
Samaria in 312 B.C., and carried away a large number of prisoners.[3] Some years later, in 296 B.C.,
Demetrius Poliorcetes did the same. When Hellenism
was triumphant throughout the East, and particularly during the reign of Antiochus Epiphanes (175–
163 B.C.), giving rise to the Jewish revolt of the Maccabees, the Samaritans, in 166 B.C., made the offer
to the Seleucid king to dedicate the temple on Gerizim to Zeus Xenios.[4] They were by this means able
to escape persecution, but not to avoid disaster, for
when the Maccabees under John Hyrcanus took
Samaria, the temple on Gerizim was destroyed and
the ancient capital of Israel sacked (*c.* 108 B.C.).[5] It

---

[1] Ricciotti, *Histoire d'Israël*, II, p. 194; Abel, *Histoire de la Palestine*,
I, p. 13.

[2] The successors of Alexander.

[3] Abel, *op. cit.*, p. 31.

[4] This tradition is in Josephus, *Jewish Antiquities*, XIII, 5, 3. For
another version cf. II Mac. 6.2; Abel, *op. cit.*, p. 123. The title *Zeus
Xenios*, Jupiter Hospitalis, is changed to *Zeus Hellenios* in Josephus.

[5] Abel, *op. cit.*, pp. 211, 217. The date is undecided. Abel places it
in 108–7 B.C., J. W. Crowfoot, *The Buildings at Samaria*, p. 30, places
it between 111 and 107 B.C., Ricciotti, *Histoire d'Israël*, II, p. 195
suggests 108–7 B.C. *The Westminster Dictionary of the Bible*, 528, adheres
to 128 B.C.

was never to recover anything of its prestige until the coming of the Romans.

Archaeology has enabled us to distinguish certain important architectural features belonging to the Hellenistic period. As we have seen, it was a period

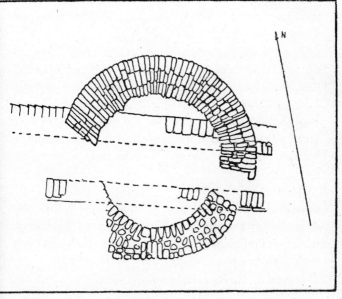

XXV. Tower of the Hellenistic Period (from Crowfoot, The Buildings at Samaria, Pl. III)

marked by important historical events. Hence it is not surprising that the excavated buildings and constructions should be connected with military requirements.

In 1933 Crowfoot's expedition uncovered an imposing round tower[1] (fig. XXV), similar to the two uncovered by the Harvard expedition[2] and which had been assigned by the latter to the time of Jeroboam II. It was in a splendid state of preservation (nineteen courses of blocks were still undisturbed), and presents the finest example of Hellenistic construction known to us to-day in Palestine.

The second important construction which calls for notice is a fortress, formerly called 'the Greek fort',[3] the citadel of the city, on the site of the ancient acropolis. Lower down, on the slope, the main city wall formed the external line of defence. It had survived all the destructions, especially in the neighbourhood of the great west gate of which we shall speak later.

Although the dating of this construction no longer presents a problem, this is the most that can be said. It is equally possible that the towers may have been built by Perdiccas who restored Samaria before his death (d. 321 B.C.), or that they were erected in the

[1] Crowfoot, *The Buildings at Samaria*, p. 25 and Plates III and XXXVI.

[2] *HES*, p. 118; plans 2, 5; Plates 28b, 29b, 30c, d, e. On the plan the two towers are situated at the south-west angle of the old Israelite palace. The diameter of one of the towers is 14 m. 70.

[3] 'The Greek Fort Wall' is the designation in *HES*. As against what Crowfoot, *op. cit.*, p. 28 and Vincent, *RB*, 1946, p. 592, have written, we have not found a 'Greco-Babylonian Fort'. The Harvard archaeologists did not go beyond describing the Babylonian constructional technique of unburnt brick used in building the walls (*HES*, p. 127).

course of the restoration of the destruction caused, either by Ptolemy Soter (312 B.C.) or by Demetrius Poliorcetes (296 B.C.)[1]. The time called for great vigilance, and the importance of the buildings carried out to strengthen the defences of the city explains why John Hyrcanus was only able to capture the city after a siege of a year's duration.[2] Its fall ended a period of the greatest prosperity during two centuries of Hellenistic civilization: the extent and varied character of western influence are illustrated by its coinage (Ptolemaic and Seleucid), the hundreds of Rhodian stamped jar-handles,[3] the Greek pottery, and even the Corinthian capitals.[4] Already the ancient capital had taken on the characteristics of western civilization. Rome, in its turn, was about to enter and invest it even more distinctly with the stamp of an alien civilization.

[1] Crowfoot, *op. cit.*, p. 27. According to Miss Kenyon the 'Fort Wall' was built about the middle of the second century B.C., as indicated by the Rhodian jar-handles.

[2] Abel, *Histoire de la Palestine*, I, p. 217.

[3] Crowfoot, *op. cit.*, p. 24.

[4] D. Schlumberger, 'Les formes anciennes du chapiteau corinthien en Syrie, en Palestine et en Arabie', in *Syria*, XIV (1933), pp. 283–317, thinks that a Corinthian capital of the Hellenistic period can be distinguished at Samaria (pp. 303–4 and Plate XXXII, 3).

IV

SAMARIA
IN THE ROMAN PERIOD

ALTHOUGH the punishment inflicted on Samaria by
John Hyrcanus had not caused the site to be abandoned, nevertheless it was not until the arrival of the
Romans that the city regained something of its former life. In 63 B.C., Pompey had annexed the district
and made it a part of the Roman province of Syria.
The city was liberated, and made 'an independent
unit of the Jewish State'.[1] A few years later, the pro-
consul Gabinius (57–55 B.C.), who had been set over
the province of Syria, not only crushed the Has-
monaean revolt, centred at the Alexandrion,[2] but
also undertook the task of restoring the ruined Hellen-
ized cities. Hence Samaria became the object of his
attentions, and its inhabitants, doubtless as a mark
of their gratitude, styled themselves 'Gabinians'.[3]

However, what he accomplished paled before the
works which, some thirty years[4] later, Herod the

[1] Abel, *Géographie de la Palestine*, I, p. 261, 263.
[2] The modern Sartabeh, on the right bank of the Jordan.
[3] Abel, *op. cit.*, p. 291.
[4] In 26 B.C., according to Abel, *op. cit.*, p. 369 and n. 2.

Great, having become king of Palestine by the favour of Augustus, decided to embark upon at Samaria, as also in many other cities of his kingdom. The new king dedicated the city to Augustus, giving it the name of *Sebaste*,[1] and on the very site of the palace of Omri and Ahab, he built a temple which he dedicated to his patron. The Idumean knew how to be all things to all men.

Henceforth Samaria was to be a Roman city (fig. XXXII), not only rivalling, but far surpassing the Israelite city. It was to contain all that western civilization expected to find at the heart of a great city: temples, a theatre, a forum, colonnaded streets, a stadium. All this was bounded by an enclosure which did not cramp the city, but rather provided it with ample residential space, well planted with trees. Here, not only the descendants of the ancient inhabitants, but also the six thousand veterans, Galatians, Thracians, and Germans, settled by Herod, lived side by side. Samaria was evidently destined to be the home of a mixed population.

The Herodian buildings[2] which had no doubt suffered damage during the first Jewish revolt (A.D. 66–70),[3] were not only restored, but also greatly in-

---

[1] The Greek rendering of the Latin *Augustus*. The name has been preserved up to our day in the modern *Sebastiyeh*.

[2] Josephus mentions them in *The Jewish War*, I, XXI, and describes them in *Jewish Antiquities*, XV, 8, 5.

[3] The rebels sacked the city in the first months of the revolt, in A.D. 66.

creased during the period of the Antonines and the
Severi, i.e., during the second and third centuries A.D.
It is sometimes very difficult to distinguish between
the periods on a site where the various buildings lie
intermingled one above the other, and the levels are

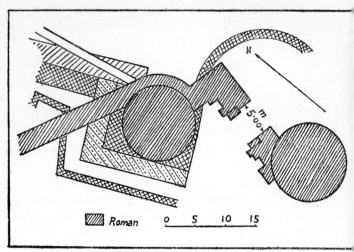

XXVI. The West Gate (from Syria, *1925, p. 325)*

not clearly defined.[1] It is easy to understand how
changes in proposed datings are bound to arise as
one expedition succeeds another, and even in the
opinion of the experts in the course of the same ex-

[1] Photographs of the excavation will give some idea of the difficulty. A few will suffice to illustrate the problems which confronted
the archaeologists. See, for example, *HES*, Plate 2a and Crowfoot,
Plate LXII.

pedition. It is, however, agreed that, with the exception of the great temple dedicated to Augustus, and one of the periods of the stadium, which go back to Herod the Great, most of the 'Roman' remains still visible at Samaria belong to a more recent period, lying between A.D. 180 and 230[1] i.e. during the reigns of the emperors Commodus, Septimius Severus, Caracalla, Heliogabalus, and Alexander Severus. At any rate, the great wave of prosperity experienced by the city after it had become a Roman colony with the name Lucia Septimia Sebasté,[2] happened during the reign of Septimius Severus (A.D. 193–211). This was its most brilliant period, according to the testimony of those of its stones which still stand,[3] or are in the course of being uncovered.[4]

The two expeditions have succeeded in tracing out accurately the line of the enclosure, about four thousand yards in length, and containing an area of about 160 acres.[5] The greatest length, from east to

[1] Crowfoot, *op. cit.*, p. 36.

[2] Crowfoot, *op. cit.*, p. 36; Abel, *Géographie de la Palestine*, II, p. 446. According to Père N. Van der Vliet, in *RB*, 1950, p. 126, the full official title was *Colonia Luciana Septimia Severiana Sebasté*.

[3] On a coin with the name of Julia Soaemias, the mother of Heliogabalus (ob. A.D. 222), there appears a tetrastyle temple with a triangular pediment (cf. *RB*, 1950, p. 125 and Plate III, 26). Three deities in the interior of the temple do not seem to have been identified.

[4] For instance, the recently discovered statue of Apollo, almost life-size, *BA*, 1953, p. 6.

[5] The rampart of the Israelite city only enclosed about twenty acres.

west, measured about two-thirds of a mile. The only gate, still visible and uncovered, was on the west. It was flanked by two round towers (Plate 7 and fig. XXVI), remarkably resembling those uncovered in

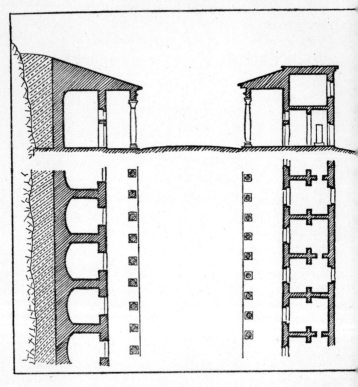

XXVII. Street with Porticos and Shops (from Crowfoot, op. cit., p. 51)

[106]

the centre of the city,[1] belonging to the Hellenistic period. However, some 'Roman' construction has been recognized.[2] A third tower, flanking the rampart, was uncovered about sixty yards further west.

Within the gate, an altar stood on the left, from which there ran a long colonnaded street (Plate 8) from west to east.[3] It has been uncovered for more than nine hundred yards, and was about fourteen yards wide, bordered by a double portico, on to which a line of shops opened, after the fashion of the stalls of modern oriental streets, laid out differently according to whether they were on the north or the south side of the street (fig. XXVII). The Corinthian capitals which crowned the columns of dark limestone,[4] suggest by their style the second phase of the Roman period, at the end of the second and the beginning of the third century A.D.

In the centre of the city stood the temple built by Herod and dedicated to Augustus[5] (fig. XXVIII). It had been built above the Israelite palaces. The north side of this imposing sanctuary consisted of a large

[1] See above p. 100. On Crowfoot's plan (Plate 1) one of the towers of this gate is marked 'Hellenistic', although, on p. 36, the gate is assigned to the Roman period (between Vespasian and Constantine). Tower 1 on the same plan is assigned to the Herodian period.

[2] *HES*, plan 10. This dating is accepted by Crowfoot, *op. cit.*, p. 36; Watzinger, *Denkmäler Palästinas*, II, p. 52.

[3] Crowfoot, *op. cit.*, pp. 50–2.

[4] About six hundred have been found, Crowfoot, *op. cit.*, p. 37.

[5] *HES*, plan 9; Crowfoot, *op. cit.*, Plates IX–X; Watzinger, *op. cit.*, Plate 9, pp. 48–9.

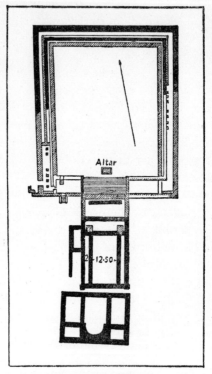

Altar

2 ← 12·50 →

XXVIII. The Temple of Augustus (from Watzinger,
Denkmäler Palästinas *II, Pl. 9*)

court, roughly square (80 yards by 80 yards), enclosed by several concentric walls. From this court the way led by a splendid staircase (Plate 9) 30 yards wide, consisting of two flights of steps, separated by a landing, to the temple proper. This would seem to have consisted of an antecella and a cella (15 yards in width), enclosed by two long and narrow corridors.

This sanctuary was surrounded by other buildings on the south and west. One of them may have been a priests' house. The other, a tripartite building, with a central hall with an apse, seems to have been connected with the cult of the emperor.[1]

An altar stood at the foot of the grand staircase, measuring 4 yards by 2 yards by 1 yard 1 foot, and surrounded by votive pillars belonging to the imperial period. A badly damaged statue, possibly representing Augustus, was found on the steps.

Further to the north, in the same sector, a second large temple[2] had been erected, and documents discovered in it made possible the recognition of two stages. In a rectangular *temenos* measuring 95 by 50 yards,[3] oriented east and west, it was possible to distinguish the plan of the rectangular temple, measuring 40 by 17 yards, but not the arrangement of its

---

[1] Watzinger, *op. cit.*, p. 50.

[2] Sukenik in Crowfoot, *op. cit.*, pp. 62–7.

[3] Watzinger, *op. cit.*, gives other dimensions: 122 yards by 44 yards, differing from those given by Hennequin, *Fouilles en Palestine*, in *Dictionnaire de la Bible*, col. 391: 110 yards by 55 yards.

interior. The whole area showed signs of having been much worked over.

Among the numerous finds, mention should be made of a Greek inscription (a dedication to Serapis and Isis), an octagonal pedestal (dedicated to Koré), two reliefs (fig. XXIX) decorated with a conical cap

XXIX. Reliefs from the Temple of Koré (from RB, 1936, Pl. VI facing p. 222)

surmounted by an eight-pointed star (the symbol of the Dioscuri),[1] and fragments of a statue of Artemis (?).

It seems very likely that on this site there was a temple of Isis built in the Hellenistic period, destroyed

[1] These reliefs have been made the subjects of a special study by Père Vincent, 'Le culte d'Hélène à Samarie' in *RB*, 1936, pp. 221–32. Cf. also M. Narkiss, 'A Dioscuri Cult in Sebastiya' in *PEF.QS.*, 1932, pp. 210–12,

by John Hyrcanus about 125 B.C., restored in the Roman period, and this time dedicated to Koré.[1] Turning back towards the ancient palaces, we reach the theatre.[2] This lies mid-way between the temple of Koré and the forum. Its plan has been completely traced out. Six steps gave access to seven blocks, divided into an 'orchestra' (fourteen rows), and a 'balcony'. The whole had a diameter of seventy yards. It had been built with the greatest care and of the finest materials. The date suggested for it is the third century A.D.

Proceeding eastward, we come to the basilica and the forum (Plate 10). The former, according to the Roman custom,[3] was devoted to public business: trade, commerce, banking, law. One of its main purposes was to house judges and litigants. It was built in the Herodian period, and consisted of a long rectangle (74 by 35 yards), divided into three naves by two Corinthian colonnades (fig. XXX). On the north side the tribunal consisted of four seats arranged in a semi-circle.[4] The building was completely restored under Septimius Severus (A.D. 193–211).

The forum was laid out adjacent to the east wall of the basilica. It was not a natural terrace,[5] but an

---

[1] Sukenik, *op. cit.*, pp. 66–7.

[2] Crowfoot, *op. cit.*, pp. 57–62 and Plates LVI–LVIII.

[3] I. Guadet, art. 'Basilique', in 'Daremberg-Saglio' *Dictionnaire*.

[4] Photos of the site before and after the excavation, in *HES*, Plates 47–51. Description on pp. 213–19. A critical study and interpretation in Watzinger II, pp. 95–7.   [5] *HES*, p. 211.

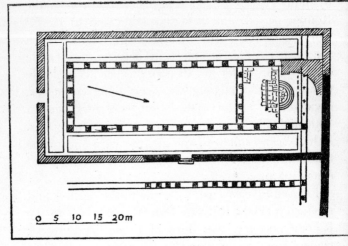

XXX. The Basilica (from Watzinger, op. cit., Pl. 14, fig. 36)

artificial platform,[1] to-day occupied by the threshing-
floors of the peasants of Sebastiyeh. It was a rectangle
(140 by 80 yards), surrounded on all four sides by a
colonnaded portico, built on a slightly lower level
(about 3 feet) than the basilica. It may have been
founded either by Gabinius, or by Herod the Great;[2]
the colonnaded portico was added much later, towards the end of the second century A.D.

The last important building is the stadium, which
the American excavators had previously identified as

[1] Crowfoot, *op. cit.*, p. 55 and Plate LI, 1.
[2] Crowfoot, *op. cit.*, p. 56.

[112]

a 'hippodrome'.[1] The Herodian wall included this imposing building (250 by 60 yards) within the city limits.[2] The excavators were obliged to content themselves with a few soundings and the exploration of the north portico. But they were able, at least, to determine that there had been two stages in the construction: the first was characterized by a Doric style, and might be attributed to Herod; the second was Corinthian in character, and belonged to the second century. A portico of twenty columns on the short sides, and of sixty-five on the long sides, surrounded the area reserved for the games and for various sports. This measured 210 by 62 yards.[3] It is somewhat strange that there is no literary allusion to the games at Samaria, since we know that Herod instituted games at Caesarea and at Jerusalem, and that other Palestinian cities (Ascalon, Scythopolis, Gaza, Neapolis) are mentioned in this connection.[4] Yet the stadium at Samaria was one of the most magnificent,[5] and the silence of the sources is hard to explain.

It should be remarked that in this sector there was

---

[1] *HES*, p. 219.

[2] Figures are those of the American excavators. Crowfoot, *op. cit.*, p. 41, gives 250 by 66 yards, but also 225 by 74 yards 'from wall to wall' (p. 42).

[3] The stadium of Miletus was of the same length, but half the width (210 by 31 yards). Figures in Crowfoot, *op. cit.*, p. 48.

[4] Crowfoot, *op. cit.*, p. 49, n. 1.

[5] 160 shafts of columns have been counted, Crowfoot, *op. cit.*, p. 37. Pictures of the stadium, Plates XLVI–L.

H

discovered a statue of a goddess,[1] identified with Koré, and that a number of dedications to the same deity have been found.[2] Various altars also have been discovered. It is not, however, legitimate to conclude that the 'stadium' was really a temple.[3] It merely shows the extent to which the whole of life, including the games in the stadium, was permeated by religion[4]

Since the city of Samaria had been provided with all the buildings considered necessary by western civilization, it is not surprising that one of the most vital necessities of civilization should have received due attention, namely, the water supply. In the Israelite period, people had to be content with what was stored in the cisterns, which left them at the mercy of bad years, that is, the years when the winter rains were poor and insufficient. That is the tragedy of the East, and a problem which is as urgent to-day as of old. The ancient city-dwellers sought by every means to avoid the uncertainty caused by the irregularity of rainfall. The excavation of Samaria has revealed how much had been done to achieve this

---

[1] Crowfoot, in *PEF.QS.*, 1933, Plate II, reproduced in *RB*, 1947, Plate VI, 3.

[2] On one the inscription runs: 'The only god, Lord of all, the great Koré, unconquered.' The title 'great', given to the deities of death, as F. Cumont has pointed out, was also given to the famous Diana of the Ephesians, Acts 19.28.

[3] Watzinger, *op. cit.*, II, p. 32.

[4] We may recall what St Paul wrote: 'Know ye not that they which run in a racecourse run all, but one receiveth the prize? Even so run, that ye may obtain.' (I Cor. 9.24.)

end. The outlet of an aqueduct was discovered, in
1931, under the south portico of the forum, and its
course was followed for 110 yards. It was partly built
and partly cut out of the rock. It has been ascertained
that the water came from the spring of 'Ain Harun,
near the modern village of Nakura, and that it was
brought to the city by an aqueduct about three miles
long, a splendid piece of hydraulic engineering, for
it involved negotiating a depression of over 65 yards,
which would certainly necessitate the building of a
bridge. To-day, near the village mosque, a spring[1]
yields abundance of very cool water, a boon which
is doubly appreciated when working in the ruins in
the great heat.

In comparison with our knowledge of the buildings
and amenities intended to provide for the needs of
the living, we know little about the arrangements for
the disposal of the dead. A great hypogeum of the
Roman period,[2] represents the majestic but peaceful
aspect of the *domus aeterna* of the time. Two burial
chambers open from the angle of an atrium, each
with eight *loculi*. The entrances to the two burial
chambers were closed by two stone slabs, carved on
the outside to give the appearance of wooden shutters.
The bodies had been laid in stone sarcophagi.[3] Five

[1] This arrangement only goes back to 1925. The water comes
from Wadi Amir, near Nakura.

[2] Sukenik in Crowfoot, *op. cit.*, pp. 81–90, Plates LXXX–LXXXI.
The tomb is E. 220, assigned to the end of the second or the beginning of the third century A.D.   [3] Ten have been found.

busts, whose rude execution contrasted with the excellence of the architecture, were found in the debris which choked the atrium. This burial chamber lay outside the city on the east, where other burials, of the same period but of less importance, were examined. One of them, however, calls for notice, with its cupola supported on matched piers.[1]

Lastly, mention should be made of the Roman *columbarium*,[2] hewn out in the rock. Six yards in height, it had ten rows of niches, providing a resting-place for the ashes of more than 250 dead.[3] Hence it would appear that inhumation and incineration existed side by side during the Roman period.

Such accurate knowledge of the kind of city Samaria was, gives colour to the episodes in the Gospel narratives in which the Samaritans play a part. It makes it easier to understand why the Jews who remained faithful to Jahvism refrained from entering a city so permeated by paganism, and why so deep a hostility should have divided inhabitants of the same country, subject to the same Roman occupation under the procurators. The Galileans shared the same feeling, and when they had to go up to

[1] This is one of the earliest examples of a dome on pendentives. The tomb was partially excavated by the Harvard expedition, *HES*, pp. 220–3. Cf. R. W. Hamilton, 'The Domed Tomb at Sebastiya', in *QDAP*, 1938, pp. 64–71.

[2] A funerary building intended to hold the urns containing the ashes of the dead.

[3] If our calculations are correct, 272, according to the data furnished by Sukenik, *op. cit.*, p. 90.

Jerusalem, rather than take the direct road, preferred to pass through Peraea (fig. XXXIII), which, like their own province, was ruled by Herod Antipas.

Hence it was not advisable to pass through Samaria in order to go up to Jerusalem from Nazareth. Those who did pass through were not always welcome,[1] nevertheless, on several occasions Jesus did not hesitate to show that he did not share the feelings of his fellow-countrymen. He even used the Samaritans as an example. When he healed the ten lepers, the only one who returned to give thanks was a Samaritan.[2] Or when it was a question of succouring the unfortunate man who had fallen among thieves on the road to Jericho, Jesus pointed out that it was neither a priest nor a Levite, representatives of the official cult at Jerusalem, but a Samaritan who showed mercy on him.[3]

Nor was this all. It was, as O. Cullmann has remarked, the meeting between Jesus and the Samaritan woman at Jacob's well[4] (fig. XXXI) which marks the foundation and beginnings of the Christian missionary movement, a movement which actually started in Samaria.[5] It is significant, too, that the

[1] Luke 9.53, where the Samaritans refused to receive Jesus and his disciples.

[2] Luke 17.16.   [3] Luke 10.33.

[4] The locality has been identified with certainty in the plain of Shechem, at the foot of Mount Gerizim. It is one more regrettable case of a sacred place being enclosed in a church.

[5] O. Cullmann, 'Samaria and the Origins of the Christian Mission' in *The Early Church* (1956), pp. 185–192.

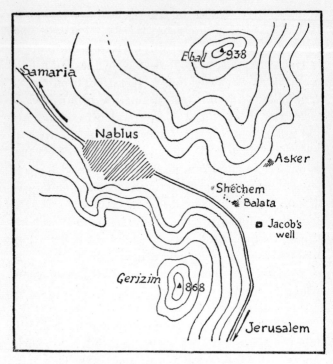

XXXI. Gerizim and Jacob's Well

missionary movement should have originated with
the Hellenists, and with Philip in particular.[1] It was
fitting that Hellenists should carry the gospel to the
Samaritans since they, like the Samaritans, were

---

[1] O. Cullmann, *loc. cit.*, p. 190, quotes Acts 8.1 and 4. The Hellenists
were Jews who had lived outside Palestine and spoke Greek.

opposed to the worship carried on in the Temple.[1] It may be added that by their composition and by their culture, already deeply influenced by western civilization, the Hellenists were the better able to understand, and, more important still, to be understood by, an environment shaped by centuries of Greco-Roman civilization. The rapidity of their success is clearly shown by the Biblical records.[2]

A notable convert was Simon the magician, whom his fellow-countrymen credited with powers nothing less than divine.[3] It is extremely probable that this individual was the priest of Koré[4] and the Dioscuri, evidence of whose cult at Samaria is provided, as we have seen, both by a temple and by monuments.

[1] O. Cullmann, *loc. cit.*, p. 191.

[2] Acts 8.6–8.

[3] Acts 8.10. 'This man is the power of God, which is called Great'. This is the very title which, as we have seen, was applied to Koré. See above p. 114, n. 2.

[4] Koré will be the Helen mentioned by Justin Martyr in connection with Simon, the Gnostic magician, who may most probably be identified with the Simon of the narrative in Acts. For these resemblances and identifications, see Vincent in *RB*, 1946, pp. 227–32.

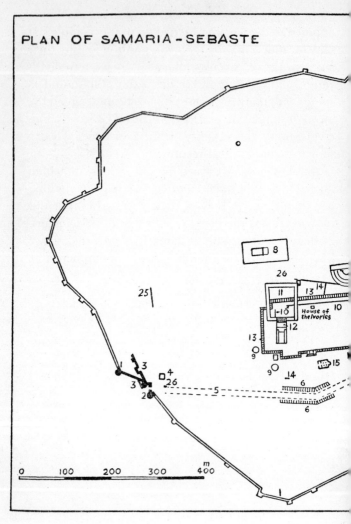

PLAN OF SAMARIA – SEBASTE

8

26

11   13 14

25

1 10
House of
the Ivories

13

12

1-10

13

9

9   14

1

3

3

4

26

15

2

5

6

6

0   100   200   300   400 m

1

X

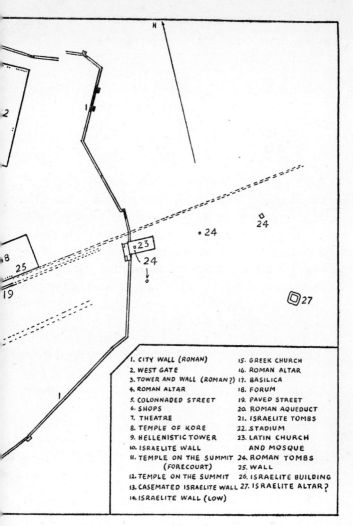

N

• 24

□ 24

○ 23
○ 24
↓
o

□ 27

1. CITY WALL (ROMAN)	15. GREEK CHURCH
2. WEST GATE	16. ROMAN ALTAR
3. TOWER AND WALL (ROMAN?)	17. BASILICA
4. ROMAN ALTAR	18. FORUM
5. COLONNADED STREET	19. PAVED STREET
6. SHOPS	20. ROMAN AQUEDUCT
7. THEATRE	21. ISRAELITE TOMBS
8. TEMPLE OF KORE	22. STADIUM
9. HELLENISTIC TOWER	23. LATIN CHURCH
10. ISRAELITE WALL	AND MOSQUE
11. TEMPLE ON THE SUMMIT	24. ROMAN TOMBS
(FORECOURT)	25. WALL
12. TEMPLE ON THE SUMMIT	26. ISRAELITE BUILDING
13. CASEMATED ISRAELITE WALL	27. ISRAELITE ALTAR?
14. ISRAELITE WALL (LOW)	

Samaria

V

SAMARIA AND
JOHN THE BAPTIST

AFTER the conversion of Constantine (A.D. 312), Christianity became the official religion at Samaria. Measures were certainly taken there to remove or to adapt to the new religion the ancient monuments of a past age.[1] However, the only remains of the Byzantine period are scattered fragments, such as the mosaic pavements found in various parts of the city, on the upper levels of the theatre, of the temple of Koré, and even of the stadium.

Nevertheless, the tradition existed at Samaria of a special regard for John the Baptist, evidenced by its veneration for the burial-place within its walls of the Forerunner. Two churches, both of Byzantine origin, were, in fact, dedicated to him.

The first stood on the site which is now occupied by the mosque, that is, on the east and on the line of the Herodian wall (fig. XXXII). The Moslem shrine has taken over a church built by the Crusaders

---

[1] According to Watzinger, *op. cit.*, II, p. 97, this is what happened in the case of the old Roman basilica. His interpretation is accepted by Crowfoot, *op. cit.*, p. 37.

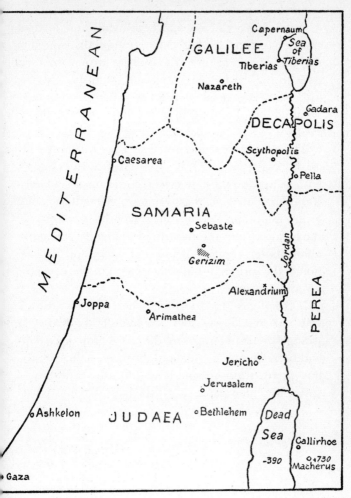

XXXIII. Palestine in the Time of Jesus

in the twelfth century A.D., where a still more ancient tradition was preserved. Three capitals, discovered in the immediate neighbourhood, bear witness by their style to the existence of a church going back to the fifth,[1] if not to the fourth century, where the tombs of Obadiah, Elisha, and John the Baptist were venerated.[2]

The second was uncovered in 1931 during Crowfoot's excavations. It was a church with three naves, with an apse on the east, oriented east and west. Greek tradition, based on the testimony of mediaeval pilgrims, maintains that it is the site of the 'discovery' of the head of John the Baptist.[3] Judging by a remarkable pilaster capital, of unusual make and decoration,[4] the original building may go back to the seventh century.

It is not easy to determine where the Forerunner was buried. The Gospel account of his death[5] is strangely silent concerning the place of his burial. It had been equally silent about the scene of the tragedy, but there is no reason to doubt the tradition of Josephus which places it at Machaerus.[6] This place,

---

[1] Crowfoot, *op. cit.*, p. 38.

[2] Abel, *Géographie de la Palestine*, II, p. 446.

[3] Crowfoot, *op. cit.*, p. 38; Abel, *op. cit.*, p. 446.

[4] Reproduced in Crowfoot, *op. cit.*, Plate LXXXV, 3 and 4.

[5] Mark 6.14–29. The Commentary of Père Lagrange, *Évangile selon saint Marc*, pp. 157–63, may be consulted with profit. The details concerning some of the traditions mentioned here have been drawn from that source.

[6] *Jewish Antiquities*, XVIII, 5, 2.

situated in Transjordan,[1] at the end of Peraea (fig. XXXIII) on the boundary of the Nabatean kingdom, dominated the Dead Sea. Herod the Great built a fortress there, enclosing a most sumptuously appointed palace, and the indispensable adjunct of a prison. Fifteen miles away, by way of contrast, the springs of Callirhoë offered their healing waters.

In such a setting of luxurious idleness we find the personages of the drama: Herod Antipas, the son of Herod the Great, tetrarch of Galilee and Peraea, his wide Herodias,[2] and her daughter Salome.[3] During a banquet given by Herod to the nobles of his court, the king, entranced by the maiden, promised to give her whatever she might desire. Salome asked for the head of John the Baptist. Bound by his oath, the king ordered the prisoner to be executed, and the bleeding head was given to the girl, who took it to her mother. The Forerunner's disciples came and took the body and buried it.

The question arises whether they buried it at Machaerus or in the immediate neighbourhood. This

[1] Abel, *op. cit.*, II, p. 371.

[2] Herodias, the grand-daughter of Herod the Great, was, in succession, the wife of a certain Herod, a person of no importance and son of Herod the Great, and the wife of Herod Antipas, also a son of Herod the Great. In other words, the niece had successively married her two uncles while both were still alive, a union forbidden by Jewish law. Mark's Gospel calls the first husband of Herodias Philip (6.17), instead of Herod.

[3] According to Josephus, Salome was the child of Herodias' first marriage.

is what might be inferred from the biblical account.
Yet the tradition preserved by Theodoret,[1] relates
that the heathen inhabitants of Sebasté opened the
chest (θήκη) of John the Baptist and burnt his
bones. Hence a transfer must have taken place, nor
is there any reason to reject the possibility.

On the other hand, according to another tradition,[2]
the head of John the Baptist was carried from Jerusalem to Cilicia, and thence to Constantinople. Now,
at Damascus, in the church of Theodosius (fourth
century A.D.), the same head was venerated, while
to-day, in the Mosque of the Umayyads, a shrine
with a marble dome is supposed to contain it.

As the result of this hasty survey, it does not appear
that any weighty reasons can be alleged against the
transference of the martyr's body from Machaerus
to Samaria. Though it may not be certain, it is not
an untenable supposition. The disciples of John the
Baptist would be likely, not only to remove their
master's body from his executioners, but also to
ensure it a secure burial. They might have found one
in Judaea, nearer home, but they chose to go further
afield to Samaria, thus avoiding Herod's jurisdiction.
It is a fact of which there can be no doubt, that, much
later, this city claimed the honour of having been
chosen as the scene of this act of reparation. It

[1] Theodoret, a Byzantine theologian, a native of Cyrrhus, north
of Aleppo (excavated by the French Institute of Archaeology at
Beirut), lived from 393 to 457.

[2] Sozomen, in *HE*, VII, 21. Quoted by Lagrange.

may be appropriate to quote here the conclusion of Flaubert's story, which vividly depicts the journey of the disciples:[1]

> The torches were extinguished. The guests departed; and Antipas was left alone in the banqueting-hall, with his hands pressed to his forehead as he gazed on the severed head, while Phanuel, standing in the midst of the great hall, with out-stretched arms, muttered prayers.
>
> As the sun rose, the two messengers previously sent by Jaokanaan[2] arrived, bringing the awaited reply.
>
> They gave it to Phanuel, who received it with ecstasy.
>
> Then he showed them the dreadful object on the dish amidst the remains of the banquet. One of the men said to him: 'Be comforted! He has gone down to announce the coming of the Christ to the dead.'
>
> At last the Essene understood the words: 'That he may increase, I must decrease.'
>
> So the three of them took the head of Jaokanaan and went their way to Galilee. Since it was very heavy, they took turns to carry it.

[1] *Herodias*. Readers who are surprised by a quotation from Flaubert in such a connection, may be referred to Jean Seznec's study of the sources of this author, of whose erudition he says that 'taken as a whole, it reveals itself as vast, minute, and accurate.' Cf. H. C. Puech's review in *RHR*, CXXXII (1946), pp. 245–7.

[2] John the Baptist.

COMPARATIVE
CHRONOLOGICAL TABLES

I

ISRAEL	JUDAH	DAMASCUS
Jeroboam I (922–901)	Rehoboam (922–915)	Hezion Tab-Rimmon
	Abijam (915–913)	
Nadab (901–900) Baasha (900–877) Elah (877–876) Zimri (876)	Asa (913–873)	Ben-Hadad I (885–855?)
Omri (876–869) Ahab (869–850) *Elijah*	Jehoshaphat (873–849)	
Ahaziah (850–849)	Jehoram (849–842)	Ben-Hadad II (Hadad-ezer) (Adad-idri) (843?)
Jehoram (849–842)	Ahaziah (842) Athaliah (842–837)	Hazael (Haza'ilu) (Mari') (ob. 801)
Jehu (842–815) Jehoahaz (815–801) Jehoash (801–786) Jeroboam II (786–746) *Hosea* Zechariah (746–745)	Joash (837–800) Amaziah (800–783) *Amos* Azariah (783–742)	Ben-Hadad III (Bir-Hadad)
Shallum (745) Menahem (745–738) Pekahiah	Jotham (742–735) Ahaz (735–715) *Isaiah*	
Pekah (737–732) Hoshea (732–724) Fall of Samaria (721)		Rezin (750–732) Fall of Damascus (732)

ASSYRIA	PHOENICIA	REFERENCES
		I Kings 12.20
		I Kings 14.20
Ashurnazirpal (883–859)		I Kings 15.33 Stele of Melqart I Kings 16.6
		I Kings 16.9–10
		I Kings 16.21, 24 Stele of Mesha
		I Kings 16.29–34; 17–22.40
Shalmaneser III (858–824)		
	Ethbaal K. of Tyre (887–856)	I Kings 22.52
		II Kings 3.1 Arslan Tash Ivory
Jehu pays tribute		II Kings 9–10, Shalmaneser's Obelisk
		II Kings 10.35
		II Kings 13.10
Adadnirari III (809–782)		II Kings 14.23
		II Kings 15.8
Tiglathpileser III (745–727		II Kings 15.10, 13
	Hiram of Tyre	II Kings 15.14 II Kings 15.23 II Kings 15.25
Shalmaneser V (726–722)		II Kings 15.30
		II Kings 17.5–6 Inscrs. of Sargon
Sargon II (721–705)		

SAMARIA	JUDAH	ASSYRIA
Samaria colonized	Hezekiah (716–687) *Micah*	Sargon II (721–705)
	Manasseh (687–642)	Sennacherib (704–681)
Samaria colonized		Esarhaddon (680–669)
	Amon	Ashurbanipal (668–631)
Samaria colonized	Josiah (640–609) *Zephaniah* *Nahum* *Jeremiah*	Fall of Nineveh (612)
	Zedekiah Fall of Jerusalem (586)	
	The Exile	
Samaria under Persian rule	Return from Exile, 1st party (537)	
Rehum governor	Zerubbabel	
	Joshua *Haggai*	
	Zechariah	
	Temple rebuilt (520–515)	

BABYLONIA	PERSIA	SELEUCIDS	EGYPT
Nabopolassar (625–605)			
Nebuchadrezzar takes Jerusalem (586) *Ezekiel*			
Nabonidus (555–538)	Cyrus (558–529)		
Fall of Babylon	Cyrus king of Babylon (538–529)		
	Cambyses (529–522)		
	Darius I (522–485)		
	Xerxes I (485–465)		
	Artaxerxes I Longi- manus (465–424)		
	Xerxes II (424)		
	Darius II Nothus (424–405)		

SAMARIA	JUDAH	ASSYRIA
Sanballat governor	Nehemiah's 1st mission	
	Nehemiah's 2nd mission	
Delaiah and Shelemiah, sons of Sanballat (407)	Arrival of Ezra (428 or 398)	
Temple on Gerizim built	Bagoas governor of Judaea	

BABYLONIA	PERSIA	SELECIDSU	EGYPT
	Artaxerxes II Mnemon (405–358) Artaxerxes III Ochus (358–338) Arses (338–335)		Elephantiné Papyri
		Battle of Issus (333)	
	Darius III Codomannus (335–330)	Alexander in Palestine (332)	

III. From the Seleucids to the Romans

SAMARIA	JUDAEA
Assassination of Andromachus	
Samaria punished (331)	
Perdiccas restores Samaria	
Ptolemy I takes Samaria (312)	
Demetrius Poliorcetes takes Samaria (296)	
	Antiochus Epiphanes (175–163) Maccabaean revolt (167)
The temple of Gerizim dedicated to Zeus Xenios (166)	
	John Hyrcanus (134–104)
The temple of Gerizim destroyed by Hyrcanus (108?)	
Pompey annexes the district (63) Samaria restored by Gabinius (57–55)	Pompey takes Jerusalem (63)
Samaria becomes Sebasté under Herod the Great (26)	

IV. PALESTINE DURING THE ROMAN PERIOD

JUDAEA–SAMARIA	GALILEE–PERAEA	BATANEA, ITURAEA TRACHONITIS, GAULAN-ITIS
4 B.C. (death of Herod) to A.D. 7	4 B.C. to A.D. 39	4 B.C. to A.D. 34
Archelaus, ethnarch	Herod Antipas, tetrarch (Mark 6.14)	Philip, tetrarch
Procurators from A.D. 7 to A.D. 41		
Coponius		
M. Ambibulus		
Annius Rufus		
Valerius Gratus		
Pontius Pilate (26–36)	Jesus crucified at the Passover of A.D. 28	34 to 37: Incorporated with the Roman province of Syria
Marcellus		
Marullus		
41 to 44: Agrippa I, king (Acts 12)	39–44: Agrippa I, king	37 to 44: Agrippa I, king
Procurators from 44 to 66		44 to 53: incorporated with Syria
Antonius Felix		
Porcius Festus (Acts 24)		
66: Jewish revolt (Titus-Vespasian)	Revolt	
132–4: Second Jewish Revolt (Hadrian)		
180: Commodus 193: Septimius Severus 211: Caracalla 218: Heliogabalus 222: Alexander Severus		

SELECT BIBLIOGRAPHY

The bibliography given here is limited to indispensable works and to important articles directly relating to our subject.

EXCAVATIONS

G. A. Reisner, C. S. Fisher and D. G. Lyon, *Harvard Excavations at Samaria* (1908–10). 2 vol. (1924). Abbreviation: *HES*.

J. W. Crowfoot, Kathleen M. Kenyon and E. L. Sukenik, *The Buildings at Samaria* (1942).

J. W. Crowfoot, Grace M. Crowfoot and E. L. Sukenik, *Early Ivories from Samaria* (1938).

It has not been considered necessary to mention here several provisional reports of excavations. For detailed information readers may consult P. Thomsen, *Die Paläs-tina-Literatur*, V, 3. pp. 478–9. For a general account of results and of the site of Samaria, see:

L. Hennequin, 'Fouilles en Palestine, Samarie', in *Dictionnaire de la Bible, Supplément* (1936).

R. W. Hamilton, *Guide to the Historical Site of Sebastiyeh* (1936.)

CRITICAL STUDIES OF THE BIBLICAL TEXTS

A. Lods, in *Bible du Centenaire* (1947).

R. de Vaux, *Les Livres des Rois*.

J. A. Montgomery and H. S. Gehman, *Kings*, ICC. (1951).

HISTORY AND GEOGRAPHY

Abel, Rev. Père, *Géographie de la Palestine*, I (1933); II (1938).
    Histoire de la Palestine, I–II (1952).

Lods, A., *Israël, des origines au milieu du VIIIe siècle* (1930); Eng. Tr. (1932).

Oesterley, W. O. E. and Robinson, T. H., *A History of Israel* (1932).

Olmstead, A. T., *History of Palestine and Syria* (1932).

Ricciotti, G., *Histoire d'Israël*, I–II (1947–8). References are to the first edition (1939).

Noth, M., *Histoire d'Israël* (1954).

Smith, G. A., *The Historical Geography of the Holy Land* (1910).

MANUALS AND GENERAL WORKS

Albright, W. F., *The Archaeology of Palestine* (1949).
    Archaeology and the Religion of Israel, third edition (1953).

Barrois, A.-G., *Manuel d'archéologie biblique*, I (1939); II (1953).

Galling, K., *Biblisches Reallexikon* (1937).

Jeremias, A., *Das Alte Testament im Lichte des Alten Orients* (1930).

Noth, M., *Die Welt des Alten Testaments* (1953).

Unger, M. F., *Archaeology and the Old Testament* (1954).

Watzinger, C., *Denkmäler Palästinas*, I–II (1933–5).

ASSYRIAN TEXTS AND MONUMENTS

A detailed bibliography will be found in *Nineveh and the Old Testament*, pp. 94–6, and need not be repeated here. Only collections of texts are listed below:

Gressmann, H., *Altorientalische Texte zum Alten Testament* (1926).
    Altorientalische Bilder zum Alten Testament (1927).

Pritchard, J. B., *Ancient Near Eastern Texts relating to the Old Testament* (1950), especially pp. 265–301.
    The Ancient Near East in Pictures relating to the Old Testament (1954).

Wright, G. E. and Filson, F. V., *The Westminster Historical Atlas to the Bible* (1945).

Grollenberg, L. H., *Atlas of the Bible* (1956).

CHRONOLOGY

In addition to the bibliography in *Nineveh and the Old Testament*, p. 96, the following may be mentioned:

Lewy, J., *Die Chronologie der Könige von Israel und Juda* (1929). We have followed here W. F. Albright's chronology in *BASOR*, 100 (1945), without depreciating the value of that proposed by E. R. Thiele, 'The Chronology of the Kings of Israel and Judah', in *JNES*, III (1944), pp. 137–86, or in *Vetus Testamentum*, 1954, pp. 185–95. Each system has its weak points and no particular system is completely convincing. For a criticism of Thiele's chronology, cf. A. G. Barrois in *JNES*, XIV (1955), pp. 192–5.

MONOGRAPHS, ARTICLES AND STUDIES

Alt, A., 'Die Rolle Samarias bei der Entstehung des Judenthums' (1934), reprinted in *Kleine Schriften zur Geschichte des Volkes Israel*, II (1953), pp. 316–37.

'Das Gottesurteil auf dem Karmel' (1935), reprinted in *Kleine Schriften*, II, pp. 135–49.

'Das System der assyrischen Provinzen auf dem Boden des Reiches Israel.' *ibid.*, pp. 188–205.

'Zur Geschichte der Grenze zwischen Judäa und Samaria', *ibid.*, pp. 346–62.

Der Stadtstaat Samaria (1954).

Antoine, P., 'Le Mont Garizim', in *Supplément au Dictionnaire de la Bible*, III, col. 535-61.

Cullmann, O., 'Samaria and the Origins of the Christian Mission' in *The Early Church* (1956).

Dhorme, E., *Les pays bibliques et l'Assyrie* (1911).

Diringer, D., *Le Iscrizioni antico ebraiche palestinesi* (1934).

Driver, G. R., *Semitic Writing* (1944).

Dupont-Sommer, A., *Les Araméens* (1949).

Bibliography

Dussaud, R., 'Samarie au temps d'Achab', in *Syria*, VI (1925), pp. 314-38; 1926, pp. 9-29. 'Melqart', in *Syria*, XXV (1948), pp. 205-30.

Eissfeldt, O., 'Ba'alshamêm und Jahwe', in *ZAW*, II (1953), pp. 135-49.
> *Der Gott Karmel* (1953).
> 'Samaria', in *RGG*, V, col. 97.

Forrer, E., *Die Provinzeinteilung des assyrischen Reiches* (1921).

Galling G. K., 'Der Gott Karmel und die Achtung der fremden Götter' in *Festschrift Alt* (1953), pp. 105-25.

Gurewicz, S. B., 'When did the Cult Associated with the "Golden Calves" fully develop in the Northern Kingdom?' in *Australian Biblical Review*, III (1953), pp. 41-4.

Hempel, J., 'Samaria', in *RGG*, V, col. 97-101.

Jack, J. W., *Samaria in Ahab's Time* (1929).

Jepsen, A., 'Israel und Damascus', in *AfO*, XIV, (1942), pp. 153-72.

Jeremias, J., 'Die Passahfeier der Samaritäner und ihre Bedeutung für das Verständnis der alttestamentlichen Passahüberlieferung', in *ZATW*, 59 (1932), pp. 109 ff.

Jirku, A., 'Benhadad', in *RAL*, I (1932), pp. 482-3.

Maisler, B., 'Der Distrikt Srq in den samarischen Ostraka', in *JPOS*, XIV (1934), pp. 96-100.
> 'The Historical Background of the Samaria Ostraca', in *JPOS*, XXII (1948), pp. 117-33.

Moscati, S., *L'epigraphia ebraica antica* (1951), pp. 27-39.

Nagel, G., 'Samarie à l'époque israëlite', in *Revue de Théologie et de Philosophie*, 17 (1929), pp. 274-93.

Noth, M., 'Das Krongut der israelitischen Könige und seine Verwaltung,' in *ZDPV*, 50 (1927), pp. 211-44.
> 'Der Beitrag der samarischen Ostraka zur Lösung topographischer Fragen', in *Palästina Jahrbuch* (1932), pp. 54-67.

O'Doherty, E., in *Catholic Biblical Quarterly*, XV (1953), pp. 24-9.

Rowley, H. H., 'Sanballat and the Samaritan Temple', in *BJRL*, Sept. 1955.

'Nehemiah's Mission and its Background', in *BJRL*, March 1955, pp. 528–61.

Sukenik, E. L., 'An Israelite Gem fron Samaria', in *PEF.QS*, 60 (1928), p. 51.

'Inscribed Hebrew and Aramaic Potsherds from Samaria', in *PEF.QS*, 65 (1933), pp. 152–6.

'Inscribed Potsherds with Biblical Names from Samaria', *ibid.*, pp. 200–04.

'Paralipomena Palestinensia, Stamped Jar-Handles', in *JPOS*, 1934, pp. 178–84.

'Potsherds from Samaria inscribed with the Divine Name', in *PEF.QS*, 68 (1936), p. 37 f.; *PEQ*, 1937, p. 140 f.

'Note on a Fragment of an Israelite Stele found at Samaria', in *PEF.QS*, 68 (1936), p. 136.

Thompson, J. A., 'Extra-Biblical Data and the Omri Dynasty', in *Australian Biblical Review*, III (1953), pp. 25–40.

De Vaux, R., 'La chronologie de Hazaël et de Benhadad III, rois de Damas', in *RB*, 1934, pp. 512–18.

'Les prophètes de Baal sur le Mont Carmel', in *Bulletin du Musée de Beyrouth*, V (1941), pp. 7–20.

'Le schisme religieux de Jéroboam I', in *Angelicum*, XX (1943), pp. 77–91.

Vincent, A., *La religion des Judéo-Araméens d'Éléphantine* (1937).

Vincent, L. H., 'Le culte d'Hélène à Samarie', in *RB*, 1936, pp. 221–32.

Review of *HES*, in *RB*, 1925, pp. 436–41.

Review of Crowfoot, *Early Ivories*, in *RB*, 1939, pp. 633–7.

Review of Crowfoot, *The Buildings* etc., in *RB*, 1946, pp. 589–94.

'Les épigraphes judéo-araméennes postexiliques', in *RB*, 1949, pp. 274–94.

Bibliography

Vriezen, T. C. and Hospers, J. G., *Palestine Inscriptions* (1951), with a chapter on the Samaria Ostraca.

Other articles consulted have been mentioned in the footnotes. Their omission here is merely due to limitations of space.

ABBREVIATIONS

AfO	Archiv für Orientforschung
BASOR	Bulletin of the American Schools of Oriental Research
BJRL	Bulletin of the John Rylands Library
JNES	Journal of Near Eastern Studies
JPOS	Journal of the Palestine Oriental Society
HES	Harvard Excavations at Samaria
PEF.QS	Palestine Exploration Fund Quarterly Statement
PEQ	Palestine Exploration Quarterly
RAL	Reallexikon der Assyriologie
RB	Revue Biblique
RGG	Die Religion in Geschichte und Gegenwart
RHR	Revue de l'Histoire des Religions
ZAW	Zeitschrift für die Alttestamentliche Wissenschaft
ZDPV	Zeitschrift des Deutschen Palästina-Vereins